Contents

The Stage Directions Guide to Getting and Keeping Your Audience

Edited by

Stephen Peithman

Neil Offen

HEINEMANN
Portsmouth, NH

For all those in front of the lights and behind the scenes
who understand the magic of theater

HEINEMANN
A division of Reed Elsevier Inc.
361 Hanover Street
Portsmouth, NH 03801–3912
http://www.heinemanndrama.com

Offices and agents throughout the world

*The editors and publisher wish to thank those who have generously
given permission to reprint borrowed material:*

"Packing Them in at the Library" by Terri Rioux. Copyright © 1992 by
Terri Rioux. Reprinted by permission of the Author.

"Talking Them into Their Seats" by Michael E. Cafferky. Copyright ©
1993 Michael E. Cafferky. Reprinted by permission of the Author.

"Marketing to the Converted" by Nancy Rothman originally appeared
in *Theater Inform*. Reprinted by permission of the Publisher.

LIBRARY OF CONGRESS CATALOGING-IN-PUBLICATION DATA
The Stage directions guide to getting and keeping your audience /
edited by Stephen Peithman and Neil Offen.
      p. cm.
    ISBN 0-325-00113-8
    1. Theater—Public relations.   2. Theater—Marketing.
  3. Theater audiences.   I. Peithman, Stephen.   II. Offen,
  Neil.   III. Stage directions (Raleigh, No. Carolina)
  PN2053.5.S69   1999
  659.2'9792—dc21   98-55260
                                                       CIP

Editor: Lisa A. Barnett
Production: Abigail M. Heim
Cover design: Barbara Werden
Cover photo: Rob Karosis
Manufacturing: Louise Richardson

Printed in the United States of America on acid-free paper

03 02 01 00   DA   2 3 4 5

Foreword

Why do we need an audience? Aren't we on stage—or back stage—because it fills some need within us? Because we enjoy it, because we need to do it?

The fact is that we need an audience to communicate with, to give us energy, to give us feedback. We need an audience to laugh at a farce, to cry at a tragedy, to ponder a playwright's insights, to tap their feet along to a musical. We need to know an audience is *there*. We need it to applaud the cast at the final curtain or withhold its approval when the performance should have been better. Is there anything sadder than an empty theater or actors trying to summon up deep emotions before a sparse house?

The word *theater* is of Greek origin, from *theasthai*, which means to see, to view. Theater needs to be seen. So, no matter how wonderful our productions, how perceptive our directing, insightful our acting, beautiful our scenery, and evocative our lighting, our work won't mean very much if nobody comes to watch.

Before television and films, when theater stood nearly

alone among the performing arts, it was much easier to attract and keep an audience. Word-of-mouth spread easily. If that wasn't sufficient, then, perhaps, posters could be put up or advertisements placed in local newspapers.

But today those tactics generally are not sufficient. The competition is too fierce. We must do more, and that is the purpose of *The Stage Directions Guide to Getting and Keeping Your Audience.*

The editors of *Stage Directions* magazine have blended our own knowledge and experience in attracting and keeping audiences with advice and suggestions from those involved in audience development and retention in community, regional, and academic theater.

Attracting an audience begins with understanding both who your company is and who its audience could be, and why people attend—and don't attend—theatrical performances. That's where the book begins. Following are chapters on specific and varied ways to attract that audience you have described. The next section of the book is information on what you do *after* you've gotten the customer inside the theater; that is, how do you keep the audience you've attracted initially? How do you keep them wanting to come back again and again? The last section of the book looks in depth at several different theater companies and how they've overcome specific problems and managed to keep their patrons and also attract new and larger audiences. Sometimes the best way to learn is by example.

Whether your theater is new and still searching for its audience or a standby of the community with a long list of steady patrons, we hope *The Stage Directions Guide to Getting and Keeping Your Audience* provides you with the information you need to make every show a sellout.

About Stage Directions *and This Book*

The majority of material in this book is based on information that first appeared in the pages of *Stage Directions*, the "practical magazine of theater." Since 1988, *Stage Directions* has published articles on a wide variety of subject matter—not only audience development and retention, but also acting and directing, management, publicity, scenic and costume design, lighting and special effects, and much more.

During that time, we've taken a close look at almost every aspect of how to attract and keep an audience. We've put all that advice to-

gether in this book updated and revised as needed, and added intro-
ductions that help put the information into perspective.

As we do with our magazine, we'd like to hear your comments
on this book, or suggestions for future topics in our expanding library
of *Stage Directions* books. Please write to us at *Stage Directions*, 3101
Poplarwood Court, Suite 310, Raleigh, NC 27604.

Stephen Peithman, Editor-in-Chief
Neil Offen, Editor

Introduction— You Need a Plan

*I*t is a battle every theater—large or small, community, academic, church, or professional—fights at every performance: how to get people to come and watch, and how to get people to come back and watch again.

In this age when so many other forms of entertainment make claims on our time and interest, attracting an audience for a theatrical production has never been more difficult. And keeping that audience has become, perhaps, even more problematic.

Today, attracting and keeping an audience depends on a broad panoply of efforts—from positioning and marketing, to publicity and advertising, to community outreach and other audience-development strategies, to customer service and, of course, the quality of our productions. It demands short-term events and long-term planning. Some of these areas overlap; some also are dealt with in *The Stage Directions Guide to Publicity*.

But attracting and holding on to an audience is more than any one aspect. It is a *mindset*.

Over the last few decades, many theaters have become increasingly aware of the competition for patrons and of their onsibility to identify, find, attract, and retain audiences. They ² created a wide range of ploys designed to put a customer in a ng seat. These stratagems have included "Pay What You Can it," "Children's Night," "Bring a Can of Food Night," "Transgender it," "Singles Night," "Costume Night," and many others.

Theaters have enticed patrons by offering lectures, talks with the director, backstage tours, pretheater dinners and cocktail parties, post-theater receptions, on-site child care, transportation to the theater, and more. They have reached out to the community and given potential audiences a peek at what they do by performing in malls, schools, senior-citizen homes, public parks, and street fairs. They have made their hours more flexible, their ticket policies more adaptable, their prices—in some cases—more affordable. They have put up posters, advertised on television and radio, printed their information on placemats and matchbooks.

Once inside the playhouse, theatergoers have received a multitude of enticements to keep them coming back, including flexible season-ticket plans, special telephone hotlines, bonus shows, preordered refreshments, and other perks of patronage.

The battle to attract and keep an audience is never-ending and continuous. It must begin with an understanding of who your company is and who its audience potentially might be. Is our potential audience people who want light entertainment or serious philosophical insights? Is our audience interested in revivals of plays they saw years ago or today's cutting-edge works? Are the potential audience members newcomers to the theater or old drama hands? Are they people with a significant amount of disposable income or those who are very careful with how they spend their money?

Why would that potential audience go to the theater—or *not* go? What would make it change its mind? How do we target that specific audience—and not waste our time and money reaching those who have no interest in what we do?

The battle to attract and keep an audience must include, therefore, a carefully worked-out plan that combines a broad range of activities. Ultimately, no matter how good our productions, our theatrical success will be measured by whether that plan worked in attracting an audience and making it want to return.

GETTING YOUR AUDIENCE

*A*ny plan to increase the size of your audience begins with information. The more you know—about your own theater company, your potential audience, your broader community, the marketing means at your disposal, and other factors—the more likely you are to be successful.

Increasing your audience generally does not happen quickly. It can be a long process, and you need to understand that the steps in that process, which will be discussed in detail over the next several chapters, do not exist in a vacuum. They are a continuum, and must all work together if they are to take you closer to your ultimate goal: more ticket buyers.

1 | *What Motivates Choice of Leisure Activity*

Why do people go to the theater? What makes them choose theatergoing, say, over going to a football game or clicking the remote control from television program to television program? In fact, what makes them choose any leisure activity rather than being couch potatoes?

Before you can learn how to entice audiences to your theater, it's useful to understand, in general, why people choose any leisure activity.

The Factors That Influence

A recent Leisure Trends/Gallup study uncovered those factors that most influence Americans in their choice of leisure activities. The findings should cast some light on how to attract audiences.

The study defines *leisure* as anything a person does for pleasure when not working or sleeping, and it involved five thousand Americans aged sixteen and older. They were interviewed to identify what motivated them in selecting leisure activities.

Not surprisingly, researchers found that "Americans are basically homebodies who prefer sitting to standing, being entertained to entertaining, and relaxing amidst familiar and unchallenging surroundings," according to Jim Spring of Leisure Trends/Gallup. As a result, the greatest motivating force in choosing leisure activity is recuperation. According to Spring, ninety-four percent of adults would rather use their leisure to recharge their psyches. This motivation does not change much with age, he adds.

Theater certainly could be considered as a possible pastime, and the American love of musical comedy could be traced to the "being entertained . . . and relaxing amidst familiar and unchallenging surroundings." However, this doesn't say much for a wide audience for new and unconventional works.

Some of the findings of the study cast light on volunteerism as well. For example, ninety-six percent of those asked said they have a strong tendency to finish what they start. This indicates that a person who makes a commitment to a new activity (such as volunteering to work back stage) is likely to stick with it.

Most Americans also think of themselves as hands-on, practical people. About eighty-one percent say they are motivated to work with their hands—again, good news for theaters who use volunteers in such production areas as sets and costumes.

Social needs are also important. According to the study, the younger we are, the more sociable we are, but the desire to be with other people remains strong for most people up to age fifty-five, when it begins to decline. Combine recuperation with socializing and you may have a good sales pitch for coming to see your company.

Our Puritan heritage shows itself in several of the study's findings. For example, most people don't seek pleasure for its own sake—it seems to make us feel guilty. However, those aged sixteen to twenty-four and those over sixty-five seem to be more strongly motivated by this need. Americans think of themselves as realists, and very few say they pick leisure activities because they're "escapist."

In summary, then, "Most Americans are recuperators in their spare time, they prefer to relax instead of achieve, and they gravitate toward familiar activities and those learned when they were young," Spring says. The last six words in that sentence should give added support to those who believe that the effort to get children involved in theater—as audience members or active participants—is the surest, long-term method to increasing theater patronage.

2 | Why Audiences Don't Come

It's helpful, of course, to know why audiences do come to the theater, but perhaps we can learn as much from why they don't *come. This knowledge may help you make changes in your marketing strategies that can boost attendance.*

How the Public Participates in the Arts

A recent report casts interesting light on public participation in the arts. The report, *Americans and the Arts*, is based on a survey conducted by the National Research Center of the Arts, an affiliate of Louis Harris and Associates.

The lack of facilities and presentations and the lack of time are the key deterrents to arts attendance, the report concludes. "Lack of time" is the reason cited most often (thirty-five percent) by Americans for not attending arts performances more than they do. A larger fifty-nine percent said that lack of time prevented them from getting involved in the arts. Leisure time has shrunk, says the report, from 26.2 hours per week in 1973 to 16.6 hours per week in this study. And it's gone down even more since. Lack of time also has affected the number of people who participate actively in the arts. But that still means eleven million Americans are active in the arts.

Beyond lack of leisure time, the study indicates that there is a large untapped market for the performing arts. Tellingly, thirty-two percent of those polled said that "not very many performances are given in this area."

Other key deterrents to attendance are: "Ticket prices are too high" (twenty-nine percent). "It is too difficult to get from here to places where performances are given" (twenty-eight percent). "It is so difficult to find parking space" (twenty-three percent). "The cost of hiring a babysitter, eating out, and other costs are more than I can afford" (nineteen percent). "It is difficult to get information on what performances are being given" (seventeen percent). "Tickets are usually too difficult to obtain" (sixteen percent). And "going out at night is a real worry" (sixteen percent).

It is striking that an average of forty-five percent of the public feel that there are not enough arts presentations where they live.

"Surely, that is not a sign of a maturing cultural entity," the report says. "To the contrary, it is a clear statement that the potential of the arts in the U.S., at least at the pivotal 'live' or community level, has only been about one-half realized—in the view of those who would make up the audience of arts."

The arts have done extremely well in capturing a larger share of a shrinking market, the report concludes. "Yet, if the facilities and presentations of the arts could increase from roughly fifty percent over the next few years, the response could be of such dimensions to bring the growth rate back to what it was in the 1970s."

People feel not only that more presentations are needed in the arts, but also that "bedrock" facilities are needed. For example, thirty-one percent reported that there is no theater in their community where plays or musicals can be performed. This, the report says, is an indication that "the growth of the arts is far from over—at least in terms of the appetite of the American people for them is concerned."

3 | *Position Yourself*

In addition to understanding who the audience is, and why or why not it will come to your theater, you need to understand exactly who your company is. What does it represent? How are you perceived? What is expected of you? Then, you can start to determine how to reach the people who want what you offer.

Why You Must Create an Image of How Your Company Wants to Be Perceived

Theater people fall in love every day. Our passionate belief in and commitment to theater makes all things seem possible. Indeed, this sort of fervor is essential to the health of any theater company.

But commitment isn't enough. The most successful theater companies have learned to transform their passion into *position.*

What's *position*? In the strict dictionary sense, to position something means to put it in a particular place or location. In the marketing sense, however, *positioning* refers to a *perceptual* location. It's where your customers place you and your theater's offerings relative to those of other companies. Effective positioning, marketers say, puts you first in line in the minds of potential audience members.

Positioning is a powerful tool that allows you to create an image of how your company wants to be perceived. That's why it's so important to transform your passion into a market position. If you don't define your product or service, someone else will do it for you, and being positioned by someone else restricts your choices and limits your opportunities. Your position in the marketplace evolves from the defining characteristics of your company and its offerings. These identifiers help define yourself and distinguish your abilities as unique and different from other theaters.

Beyond Mission

Many if not most theater companies have a mission statement. But Keith Martin, of North Carolina's Charlotte Repertory Theatre, agrees that a positioning statement is better. Such a statement, according to George Thorn of ARTS Action Research, who developed the format, should include the following:

1. *A context-setting definition of the community and your work within that community.* What's the one thing you do best? What's unique about your company or your offerings? Identify your greatest strength and use it to position yourself.

2. *Your artistic mission*—why you exist, your aesthetic and philosophic vision, and who makes the decisions about this vision.

3. *A descriptive listing of all the projects, programs, and activities that fulfill your mission.*

4. *A broad list of your organizational goals*—future plans, strategies, and objectives.

5. *The criteria by which you measure success*—the most important element, in Martin's opinion.

"Be passionate in creating your positioning statement," Martin advises. "Speak in a positive voice: 'We are . . .' rather than 'We are not. . . .' Use your own voice, not that of others, or what you think others want to hear."

How do you know if you have done a good job in preparing the statement? Responds Martin: "If you removed the name of your company from your positioning statement, would you, the board, and your supporters know which organization is described?"

Questions to Answer

A positioning statement provides many benefits. It gives all members a shared understanding of what is essential about your company. It also helps you learn more about your own customer base, your competitors' offerings, and your own strengths. This allows you to design a cost-effective and highly targeted strategy to market yourself in your area.

The process itself can be beneficial. It leads to further questions that should be answered in comparison to other theaters in your area:

- Do you offer plays that your audiences want to see?
- Is your product well produced?
- What controls are in place to assure consistency?
- How do your productions look?
- How do your promotional pieces look?
- Are your ticket prices in line with what is charged in your area?
- Do you make it easy for people to purchase tickets?
- Are your staff helpful and pleasant?
- Do you make an effort to solve problems to the customer's satisfaction?
- Is it easy to find your theater?
- Are you in a good location?
- Do you go out into the community instead of making it come to you?

If the answers to any of these questions reveal problems, you can begin to solve them. If they reveal major strengths, you can move to exploit them.

Clarifying your mission is important. But positioning, when used effectively, can help you to be first in the mind of audiences. And that's a place we'd *all* like to be.

Use a Rifle, Not a Shotgun

After you've determined and clarified who your theater company is, and what it stands for, the next step is to determine who your potential audience is—and what is the most direct way of reaching them.

Targeting Is a Cost-Effective Way to Increase Audiences

J ust who is your audience and how can you best reach them? The answers to these two questions are essential to a productive—and cost-effective—marketing program.

Most theater companies or programs begin with the play. In other words, the product is designed and produced, and then we cross our fingers and hope that people will come see it.

Good marketing techniques can help at both ends of the process—choosing plays that will appeal to audiences and helping you promote your productions more effectively. Let's look at some of the basics that will help you do both.

What Is a Market?

In essence, a *market* is the set of actual and potential audience members for a season or a particular production. Let's start by defining some important concepts. The *potential market* is the set of people who profess some level of interest in a production or season. However, consumer interest alone is not enough to define the market. Potential patrons must have adequate income to afford tickets. Market size is further reduced by personal-access barriers. For example, older people may fear going out after dark, or you may be located in the city while many of your potential audience members live deep in the suburbs. Such access problems will make the market smaller. What's left is the *available market*. That portion of the available market on whom you decide to focus your efforts represents the *served market*. The *penetrated market* is your current patron base, the people who actually are coming to your shows.

To make this concept clearer, see the chart shown on page 13. The bar on the left illustrates the ratio of the potential market (here about ten percent) to the total community population. The bar on the right takes that ten percent and breaks it down further. You'll note that only a small percentage are the people you want to or can expect to reach, including current customers. (These percentages are somewhat arbitrary; your own situation may differ sharply.)

Segmenting the Market

It doesn't take much to realize that not everyone is in the market for a theatergoing experience. It may be painful to admit, but many people have absolutely no interest in the theater and never will. Of those who might attend a play, some will not attend at all or will attend a different production. Therefore, each theater must first distinguish between its potential customers and those who will never come.

Once you have estimated total market demand for your productions, look at how this market may be *segmented*—marketing talk for the presence of definable, smaller groups. Such groups might include seniors, people living in certain high-income areas, professional people, people known to attend other arts events, and so on.

Although markets can be segmented in several ways, the most useful segmentation approach will have the following characteristics:

1. The segments are *measurable*. You must be able to determine the size and characteristics of a segment. (How many people go to arts events in your area? How many professional people can you identify in your city?)

2. The segments are *accessible*. In other words, you must be able to reach the segment and serve it effectively. Certain segments are more difficult to reach than others. (Can you put together a mailing list of seniors in your area, or are there other ways to get their attention?)

3. The segments are *substantial*. Let's face it, if you're going to target an audience, it needs to be large enough to warrant the marketing

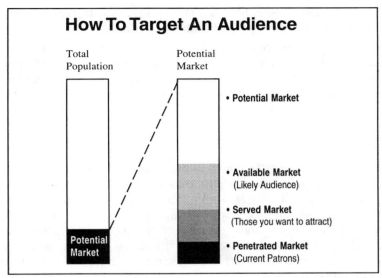

How To Target An Audience

Total Population

Potential Market

Potential Market

- **Potential Market**
- **Available Market** (Likely Audience)
- **Served Market** (Those you want to attract)
- **Penetrated Market** (Current Patrons)

The bar at left shows that only 10-20% of people in your community are likely theatergoers. The bar at right shows possible breakdown of your share of that market. Marketing is cost-effective if targeted at available and served markets.

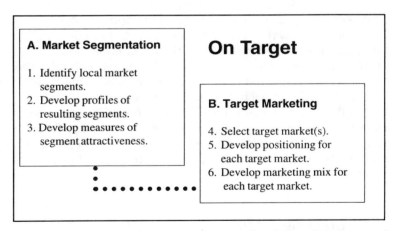

On Target

A. Market Segmentation

1. Identify local market segments.
2. Develop profiles of resulting segments.
3. Develop measures of segment attractiveness.

B. Target Marketing

4. Select target market(s).
5. Develop positioning for each target market.
6. Develop marketing mix for each target market.

To use target marketing, first divide the potential market into distinct groups of people who might require different marketing approaches, such as seniors, youth, organizations (box A). Then develop a particular approach for each group (box B).

effort. How large depends on a number of factors, including your budget, your theater size, the number of performances.

4. The segments are *durable.* Designing a successful program or season requires extensive planning time, money, and commitments from staff. You need to consider whether an identified segment will persist long enough to justify your efforts.

Target Marketing

Once you have identified the market segments that match your productions and your resources, choose one or more of those segments to focus on, and develop market offers specifically to meet the needs of each selected target group. You already may be doing this in some way—for example, with special offers to seniors, youngsters, schools, and civic groups. You also can design a season around your primary audience and a second season around a more adventurous but identifiable group.

Target marketing thus makes lots of sense. First, you can spot market opportunities better when you are aware of different segments and their needs. For example, if you have a large population of seniors, you might offer reduced prices at matinees, when they are more likely to come, or offer early evening performances.

Second, you can make finer adjustments of your programs to match the desires of the market. When you know your audiences, you have a better chance of selecting shows that will sell. And you will know better how to sell unusual productions by marketing them in terms that will appeal to your target audience.

Finally, you can make finer adjustments of prices, advertising placements, mailings, and the entire promotional mix. Instead of trying to reach all potential theatergoers with a "shotgun" approach, you can create separate marketing programs aimed at each target market—a "rifle" approach.

Two Marketing Strategies

Two types of marketing strategies emerge. *Undifferentiated marketing* is the most common approach by theater companies. You choose to ignore the different market segments and instead focus on the common needs or desires of your potential audience. You design one season or program that will appeal to the largest number of consumers. The costs of developing, offering, and marketing are all kept low through limiting efforts to one program. Of course, lower costs also are accompanied by reduced consumer satisfaction because you can't possibly meet varying wants or preferences.

Differentiated marketing operates in two or more segments of the market but designs separate programs for each. (The "second season" of experimental plays is an example of such an approach.) This lets you strengthen perceptions of your theater as a specialist in certain types of productions or services and create greater audience loyalty. Differentiated marketing is usually more costly because you have to spend more on marketing research, season development, and communications. However, it is often more cost-effective. Before going in this direction, you need to balance the likelihood of greater effect against higher costs.

Where the Audience Is

The real challenge is to entice people into your theater who haven't been there before. But how do you identify and locate people who may be prospective theatergoers?

Knowing where prospects live is important. A mass mailing to the entire community is expensive and probably won't provide good results. But a smaller mailing to an area where you already have a lot of subscribers may get you a significant response—particularly if you work with U.S. Postal Service carrier routes, which break down zip codes to specific streets and blocks of homes. If you keep a computerized list of patrons, run a report showing how many people live in each zip code. This may tell you which zip codes will be best for your mailing. Census data is also useful here; your local library should have it available. Once you know where your potential patrons live, you can check zip codes and carrier routes.

You also can target professional people, those with a college education, or people over forty for your mailings. How? Start with members of your own company. Ask them to share mailing lists from their professional organizations, alumni groups, and clubs. Census data gives less specific information, but will tell you in what areas these types of people live; you then can send a targeted mailing to households in those locations.

Sometimes what you learn about your audience leads you in an entirely different direction. For example, in "A Gem of an Idea: How the Jewel Box Sells Out" (see Chapter 38), we learn how one theater company decided to *lower* ticket prices in order to attract more people. It worked, and with no financial side effects.

Advertising

The most effective advertising is the most targeted. Once you have gone through the steps just outlined, you can expect to spend your marketing and advertising dollars much more wisely.

Placing an ad in the entertainment section of a large metropolitan newspaper may not be a wise move. Ad rates are determined by total readership of the publication, whether or not those readers have any interest in theater. Why spend large sums on a newspaper ad if you can get better results with a targeted mailing to people you know have *some* interest in theater? And if you do decide to place an ad, which newspapers do your targeted audiences read and what sections of those papers? To which radio stations do they listen? To which television stations? To which clubs or churches do they belong?

Once you have this kind of information, you can use it to make effective promotional decisions. A good source of practical tips on advertising, publicity, and promotions is George F. Chartier's *Full House* (ISBN 1-881237-00-1, Dramatics Concepts Publishing), as well as *The Stage Directions Guide to Publicity.*

Don't Forget the Core

The single most important group in your marketing efforts must be your current patrons. It is far more cost-effective to keep current audience members than to find new ones to take their place. You'll read more about keeping your current audience members satisfied in the next section of the book.

In the meantime, here are some general ideas on the subject. You can keep your core audience loyal by paying attention to them and rewarding them for their loyalty. Send them an insider's newsletter, give them a special number to call for tickets, allow them to keep seat assignments from season to season. Ask them for their birthday (month and day) so you can send them a card, perhaps with a gift certificate for refreshments at the next performance. Ask them to suggest shows for upcoming seasons. In other words, make them feel valued. They'll repay you a hundred times over with their attendance and their positive word-of-mouth.

And that is the kind of advertising you can't buy.

Yeses, Noes, Maybes, and Ineligibles | 5

*H*ere's a math problem for you: If the population of your town and the surrounding area is a hundred thousand, what size audience can your theater expect to attract? Such a question is basic to the growth and development of any theater company, but it's surprising how few theaters really know the answer.

Bradley Morison and Kay Fliehr did some extensive research into audiences during the early years of the Guthrie Theater in Minneapolis. They divided the community into four types of people: the Yeses, the Maybes, the Noes, and the Ineligibles.

The *Yeses* are those people who have made the arts a part of their life. They tend to be above average in terms of both education and income, and are the backbone of both the regular audience and the donors.

The *Maybes* are uncertain about the importance of the arts in their life. They may be interested in yet intimidated by the idea of theatergoing. If so, it may be that they are not familiar with it or feel that "culture" is only for the rich or the highly educated.

The *Noes* have consciously or unconsciously eliminated

the arts from their life. They are turned off by arts activities—they don't read or care to hear about them.

The *Ineligibles* are those people who are too old, too young, or cannot go to a theater because they are incapacitated in some way. (While arts organizations can take programs to these people, the Ineligibles are not potential audience members for most traditional theatrical events.)

Initially, Morison and Fliehr estimated that about three to five percent of the population were Yeses, twelve to fifteen percent were Maybes, thirty percent were Ineligibles, and fifty to fifty-five percent were Noes. Research carried on around the country during the past twenty-five years generally confirms their figures. Rarely does more than twenty percent of a community's population take part in the arts—the total of the Yeses and Maybes combined.

Twenty percent of one hundred thousand is twenty thousand as a potential audience, but this audience does not equal attendance. To determine attendance, you must multiply the total number of different people who attend one or more arts activities or events of any kind in a given year (marketers call this *reach*) by the average number of times during the year that they participate in arts activities (*frequency*). In other words, Reach × Frequency = Total Annual Attendance.

You can see that not every one of those twenty thousand potential audience members attends an event each year, and not all of those who do attend an event do so more than once or twice. In fact, studies indicate that most arts organizations in the United States currently reach *three percent or less* of their population, and that attendance has peaked at about this level. Therefore, if your immediate community (that is, your town or city and the surrounding area) has a population of one hundred thousand, you can expect a potential audience of about three thousand.

In their excellent book, *Waiting in the Wings: A Larger Audience for the Arts and How to Develop It* (Americans for the Arts), Morison and Julie Gordon Dalgleish write that although the arts have grown considerably in attendance and a little in reach over two decades, "they have not succeeded in moving far beyond the basic type of person who has always attended and supported them. Demographically, arts audiences are almost exactly the same as they have always been: far above the national average in education, income, and proportion of professional and managerial occupations represented. The potential size of the audience is therefore limited by the number of these kinds of people in the population."

More important, they add, as an arts organization pushes toward the edges of this demographic base, growth slows and finally stops. In essence, it runs out of potential customers. It begins to compete with other institutions for the same limited market segment.

In other words, in that community of one hundred thousand, your theater's potential audience of three thousand will have to be shared with other arts organizations in your area—ballet, symphony, art museum. And when people have choices to make, they may not choose you.

The problem is that most theater companies rely too heavily on the Yeses, even though these people form the smallest component of the available audience and may already be stretched among several different arts groups. On the other hand, when companies begin audience-development programs, they may waste their efforts trying to reach everybody in the community, even though eighty percent may be Noes or Ineligibles. Cost-effective audience development must concentrate on the Maybes—here there is the possibility for growth.

Your first step is to determine what reasons the Maybes may have for not coming to your shows. Then your course is clear: Create marketing and publicity strategies that speak directly to those concerns.

Marketing research can be complex—and expensive. To keep it cost-effective, we recommend the book, *Do-It-Yourself Marketing Research*, by George Edward Breen (Replica Books; ISBN 073510039X). Breen explains the basics without your needing a knowledge of statistics or complex formulas. He also provides sample questionnaires and explanations of how to do surveys by mail or in person.

In-Person Surveys

We don't recommend mail surveys for nonprofit theater groups. For one thing, they require a large outlay of money for printing and postage. And results are often what is termed *self-selecting*—that is, the people who complete and return the forms are likely to be the most supportive of the arts and who probably already come to your shows.

A short series of questions asked at a local shopping area is far less expensive and can give you better results, because you're more likely to get a good cross section of the community.

When doing in-person surveys, you first must weed out the Noes and Ineligibles. Ask, "Have you ever been to a live theater production or contemplated going to such a production?" If the answer is "no," send them on their way. If they reply "yes," find out if they go to the theater on a regular or semiregular basis. If so, they are a Yes. Find out what local theater groups they attend and ask their opinion about the productions they have seen. Keep it brief. Their information is valuable, but your chief interest is the Maybes. Make sure all Yeses are asked if they want to be on your mailing list.

When you have identified a Maybe, find out the reasons why they don't go to theater on a regular basis. Cost? Parking? Play selection? Don't expect people to have fully formed opinions on the spot. It's better to give them a choice of possible reasons first, then ask them if they have any additional thoughts. Don't assume you know the reasons, one way or the other; always give people a chance to express their own opinion. And be sure to give them a chance for some positive responses as well. For example, you might read a list of five options to increase audience attendance and ask them which might get them to a theater—half-price tickets for certain nights, valet parking, special family matinees, and so on.

Remember, however, that this is not a time to be selling your company. You are trying to find out what might attract or discourage potential audience members. And always keep in mind that in most cases, you are stopping people on their way to some specific destination. Keep the questions brief and to the point, and thank the respondents when you're done.

Phone interviews can be handled in much the same way. You will find, however, that many more people object to being surveyed by phone than in the open spaces of a shopping area.

Focus Groups

A focus group is a group of people—in this case, all Maybes—brought together for a discussion that may last from one to two hours. The session normally is tape-recorded or videotaped and the results transcribed and summarized. The discussion is free and unhampered, except that you designate someone to be a group leader to keep the conversation centered on the subject at hand. (It's a good idea that the group leader not be a member of your company, so that he or she doesn't unintentionally reflect any preconceived ideas to the group.)

A group should be no fewer than ten and no more than fifteen people. To put together such a group, you might contact local service clubs to help you out. A donation to the club for its time may help gain support. (It need not be money; you can give a block of tickets to be raffled off at a club meeting.)

One such session may not be enough; you need to do from two to six different groups and compare the results.

Again, *Do-It-Yourself Marketing Research* describes how to run such a group. Author George Edward Breen points out that this type of research can uncover the little things that motivate audiences either positively or negatively—matters that often go undiscovered with other types of survey techniques. You begin by explaining to the group the problem you want to address—most likely, the need for larger audiences for your productions. Come prepared with a list of possible reasons for the problem, as well as marketing strategies to overcome them, but don't restrict your group to your first thoughts— let them roam through this complex subject. Don't criticize any ideas brought up during the session. Keep the momentum going, but always have firmly in mind your need for some direction.

Here also is a chance to display your marketing pieces— brochures, flyers, posters, radio spots—and have the group review and comment on them.

Remember that a focus group is a microcosm of your potential audience. You cannot get or expect statistically valid data from such a group. Instead, you use it to probe for details that might otherwise be overlooked.

What Next?

When you have the raw information, you need to analyze it. Locate those areas of concern over which you have control. For example, those you survey may think your theater location is poor. You may or may not have the option of changing venues. If you don't, you need to find other areas of significance to your potential audience that can be analyzed and addressed through various marketing strategies. For example, if the perception is that your theater is in a "bad" part of town, you might want to stress in your marketing that you have well-lighted parking immediately adjacent to the theater or that you have early mid-week performances that get audiences out before 10:00 P.M.

If ticket price is a concern, look at ways you can introduce special pricing for certain performances. If parking is a problem, talk to nearby businesses about using their lots after business hours. If your choice of plays turns off many Maybes, consider offering at least one show a year—preferably the season opener—that is a crowd-pleaser. In any case, your research should make it clear just what direction you need to take.

6 | *Make the Most of Your Efforts*

Y ou can't market your theater company well unless you can list your selling points and your potential audiences, and then match the two lists. Here's how: First draw up a list of those qualities that make your company's productions attractive to a potential theatergoer. While every company is different, selling points might include the following:

- Your company's reputation for excellence
- An enjoyable night out at relatively low cost
- Comfortable seating
- Plenty of parking
- Social aspect of meeting others in a congenial setting
- A mix of shows for all tastes
- Live performance, not television or film
- Professional-quality performances
- Live orchestra
- New or newly refurbished theater

- Excellent acoustics
- Interpretation for hearing-impaired

Be sure to consider those unique selling points that set your group apart. Now draw up a second list, this time of potential audiences. Again, your own case may differ, but consider such possibilities as:

- Your existing audience/subscribers
- Clubs and organizations
- Schools
- Students
- Local theatergoers
- Local "new" audience, including new and long-term residents who might become theatergoers
- Theatergoers from a distance
- Special-interest groups

Drawing the Right Conclusions

Your next step is to create a matrix like the one shown on page 24. The company's selling points are listed vertically on the left and its potential audiences are listed from left to right above. The idea is to find matches between a particular selling point and a potential audience. When you find one, place an "X" in the intersecting square. If you're not sure, put a question mark. If you find something you would consider a definite or *must,* put in an "X" and circle it. This exercise helps you describe the audiences you wish to target. It works well because it provides a visual approach that makes the relationships extremely clear.

Once you've finished your chart, you'll need to estimate how many people in each target group (along the top of the matrix) will actually buy tickets. Be realistic: Use any past records you can to help arrive at an accurate figure. Be conservative in your estimates, as well. Remember, your goal is to build a steady audience of repeat customers. Without this core, your attendance figures will fluctuate too much for accurate planning.

If there is a special-interest group, you may get some kind of audience from it, but don't count on it as a steady thing. Clubs and organizations are a good source of ticket sales, particularly if you offer group rates, but any one organization cannot be counted on every time. However, if you can court a large number of such organizations,

	Existing audience	Clubs & Orgs	Schools	Students	Local new aud.	Special Int. Grp.
Company's reputation	⊗	⊗	⊗		⊗	
Enjoyable night out	X	⊗		X	⊗	X
Relatively low cost	X	X	⊗	⊗	⊗	
Comfortable seating					X	X
Plenty of parking					X	X
Social		X			X	
Mix of shows	⊗				X	
Live performance			X	X		
Professional-quality	⊗					
Live orchestra			X	X		
New theater					X	
Excellent acoustics					X	X
Interpretation for hearing-impaired						X

This simple matrix helps you determine the selling points (left) you have to offer your various potential audiences (top).

you may get a steady number from different ones. Also, sometimes the theme or subject of a particular play will suggest a one-time target audience, and that is certainly worth following up as well. Theatergoers who are not subscribers to your company are possibilities, but they may have no loyalty to your company, and so will need to be addressed frequently.

New audiences are practically impossible to quantify. They may overlap with and be contained within other groups. The problem is that you have no way of knowing what their interests may be. Some of your general publicity may draw in some of these groups, but there is no way to market aggressively and economically to them. (Again, see Chapter 5, "Yeses, Nos, Maybes, and Ineligibles.") Your task now is to figure out how many people you need to bring in at current ticket prices to:

- pay for production costs
- pay for administrative overhead
- build your savings cushion

If you have a shortfall between the income you need to generate and the amount raised by ticket sales, you have two choices: raise ticket prices or increase ticket sales. While it may seem easier to raise prices, the result is always a loss of some ticket sales, which may leave you where you were or even worse off. It all boils down to this: If you have empty seats to sell, you should be selling them. That's where the second part of the work comes in—determining the marketing activities that will fill those seats in a cost-effective manner.

The Right Piece

Not every type of marketing activity works equally well with each target audience. Below, we show a second matrix which indicates the target audiences across the top and possible marketing approaches along the left side, including a flyer, brochure, poster, display ads, direct-mail letter, phone sales, ticket discounts, group sales, personal contact, and media contacts. There may be others you want to consider. In this matrix, you are attempting to find the best way to inform each target audience why and how they should buy tickets. Mark possibilities and priorities in the same way you worked the first chart. You now have a list of possible marketing activities geared toward specific audiences.

Because your resources are not unlimited, you need to decide which of the activities will be most cost-efficient and then focus on

	Existing audience	Clubs & Orgs	Schools	Students	Local new aud.	Special Int. Grp.
FLYER		X	(X)	(X)	(X)	
BROCHURE		X	X		X	X
POSTER			X	X	X	
DISPLAY ADS					X	
DIRECT MAIL LETTER	(X)	X	X			(X)
PHONE SALES	X	X				X
TICKET DISCOUNTS			(X)	(X)		
GROUP SALES		(X)				
PERSONAL CONTACT						(X)
MEDIA CONTACTS	X				(X)	

Once you determine your target audiences, you can assess what types of marketing will work best with each group. You will need to justify the cost of each marketing effort with the expected return on investment.

them. You do this basically by drawing up and budgeting your priorities. For each marketing activity, you need to address three factors:

- how many tickets the activity is likely to sell
- whether the activity fits within your budget
- the general message the activity conveys about your group

You need to take some time to consider these issues, particularly as you deal with making best use of your limited resources. The use of a matrix can change the way you currently market your productions. For example, you may have seen a poster as a priority, but the matrix indicates that a flyer may be a better choice for reaching your core audience because they can pick it up, take it with them, read and reread it at leisure, and order tickets by mail or phone with the information provided. You may find you need more than one flyer—perhaps one for the general public and another one for students. You may have special groups, such as senior citizens, to whom a special flyer might be appropriate. Again, let the matrix guide you in brainstorming approaches to attract new audiences and keep the audiences you already have.

Reach Out and Touch Someone | 7

You've identified and quantified your potential audience. You know who you are and who they are and what they like. Now, how do you reach them? If large segments don't want to—or can't—come to you, one solution is to go to them. There are a multitude of definitions of the term community outreach, *but what they all have in common is the realization that theater companies must go beyond the traditional if they are to grow their audience. Here are some ideas on how to do that.*

Everyone Benefits When We Put "Community" Back into Community Theater

DOUGLAS LARCHE

N
ew audiences, patrons, donors, grants, materials, actors, and technicians are only some of the benefits of keeping the "community" in community theater.

Those of us in community theater think we already do this very well. We engage in membership drives and occasionally scour our communities for technicians and builders, and we all have canvassed friends and friends of friends to fill out a cast. So it may seem absurd to suggest that we may be excluding people from our circle.

But sometimes recruiting is haphazard, driven by immediate need, and populated by a close circle of friends, when we really should build and sustain ensemble. Our community theaters should be families whose members share with and respect each other. Entrenched power and personal aggrandizement have no place there.

Then there is the problem of inertia. When we finally find

a permanent performance space, we rejoice at our good fortune, consolidate all our theatrical flotsam and jetsam, and settle in for a well-deserved rest.

But we cannot rest. If we are to remain vital elements of our communities, we have to reach people. We must take theater to them. We must concentrate on outreach.

Traditional plays at traditional times in traditional settings are our lifeblood. But we can perform nontraditional shows at nontraditional times in nontraditional settings as well. And, if my experience is any guide, each time we reach out, we will find new audiences, actors and technicians, board members, and donors.

This outreach can be accomplished fairly simply through some imaginative programming and performances in nontraditional spaces.

Children's Theater

A fairly easy way to involve the community is through children's theater. It brings people in droves—many of whom have not been in a theater in years—and provides new and larger pools of actors and technicians. Royalties for children's shows are usually small, costumes frequently can be created at home, and sets often can make use of freestanding scenery (even cardboard cutouts), so they also can travel easily, going where the children are. Most important, the experience and the sense of community generated by children's theater is wonderful.

Children's classics and standard children's titles are frequently better recognized by the community than any other titles. And because of the ever-increasing catalog of shows that treat social issues, we also can contribute to a more aware and tolerant community. Interactive plays can give children a sense of participation and ownership that almost always has them coming back for more.

Compilations and Originals

I've had the opportunity to be involved with readers theater, choral reading, mime performances, puppet shows, educational theater of all kinds, talent extravaganzas, improvisational theater, and scene presentations. They all can work to benefit your company.

Compilations and original theater can be a creative outreach gold mine, whether you are creating special programs for special needs or producing the works of local authors. For Carousel Theater in Indianola, Iowa, I proposed and administered the first Prairie Play-

wright Festival, in which we solicited, chose, and produced three local original one-act plays as part of our season.

At Grand View College (Des Moines, Iowa) nearly twelve years
later, we established a five-show original summer season called "The
Prairie Playwright." In its fourth season, it attracted sixty-seven en-
tries from nine states, with one year's winner, *Mexicanville*, published
by Dramatic Publishing Company.

Low-cost, effective community theater can be found or created
for so many needs. I've worked on shows for traditional and unique
holidays (ranging from haunted houses to full-length original Christmas musicals), summer recreation programs in performance and
workshop, town and city celebrations, month-long festivals like
Black History Month, and touring self-image plays to various community settings. Each has served a particular need and gained new
awareness of theater as an entertainment source.

Odd Spaces and Places

The answers to "What can we do to reach the community?" are limited only by your imagination. So, of course, are the answers to
"Where can we do it?"

On the road to finding our own places, the groups I have worked
with have performed in the most unlikely of settings, under the most
difficult of circumstances—but each of those spaces had its own
charm and each drew new audiences. Whether it was the side of
town the space was in, the open air, the proximity to business or
school—for some reason, people came who never came before.
That's a small but vital lesson: While your hardcore audience will
come to see you without much prodding, sometimes you have to
take your magic to new audiences in order to find them.

If I were to ask a group of community-theater people to write
down the three most unusual places in which they have performed,
the list would be astonishing. My own list includes outdoor county-
fair arenas and ornate old opera houses; courtrooms and city parks;
libraries and Masonic lodges; bank-storage garages and restaurant
meeting rooms; gymnasia and auditoria; general hospitals and can-
cer wards; senior-citizen housing developments and nursing homes;
state fairs, historical buildings, and the rotunda of the state capitol;
preschools, elementary, middle, junior high, and high schools; fine
college theaters, studios, and multipurpose rooms; lounges, side-
walks, homes for the developmentally disabled, and camps for trou-
bled children; and lakesides, oceansides, and firesides.

By staging *Inherit the Wind* in the courtroom of our county courthouse, and with very aggressive marketing, our company was able to sell out six nights in little Indianola, Iowa, for this classic modern drama.

Each venue introduced theater to people who might never have seen it. Each offered unique challenges and rewards. All helped us take our community theater to our community. And all helped us gain more visibility.

So, ask yourself: What venues exist in *your* community to energize your company, find new audiences and talent, and provide service, entertainment, and culture?

A Question of Finances

Outreach programming, of course, raises the question, "How can we possibly afford it? Where can we find the funds, materials, and personnel to support these aggressive, ambitious new directions?"

It is one of life's little ironies that these new directions fly in the face of traditional wisdom. They are *investments*. They don't cost. They *pay* in dividends you might never imagine.

As you engage in outreach, you will find both broad new audiences and narrowly focused ones. You will uncover and discover new stables of talent, new workers, donations, patrons, dollars.

And not everything is as costly as you might think. As I have already pointed out, royalties for children's theater are frequently low, and many of the classics are in the public domain. Sets and costumes need not be expensive, and many works can be done in a minimalist style. For these efforts, the ticket-to-production cost ratio is particularly favorable. With patience and aggressive marketing, community support for the presentation of drama can grow and become self-supporting.

Outreach Generates Dollars

Most important, when you take theater to the people, new money sources begin to appear. New donors can be targeted and found for your efforts directed at education, the culturally disadvantaged, the physically or mentally challenged, the elderly, the migrant, the culturally diverse, the incarcerated.

This leads to more goodwill. Suddenly, individuals, organizations, and businesses who once were hesitant to spend $25 for a program ad or $50 to become a patron will donate hundreds of dollars of in-kind services, materials, transportation, advertising space, and time. Some even will underwrite you with hard cash. And unique productions targeted at new, underserved audiences make you look better and better to organizations providing grants.

Believe me, I know. I've personally been involved in writing and receiving grants for production, performance, and/or touring from three churches, two colleges, two banks, two service clubs, private businesses, a community fine-arts commission, and many other agencies—more than a quarter of a million dollars, and nearly as much in in-kind donations. Add to that tens of thousands more in donations, discounts, and gifts from everyone from local music dealers, printers, and hardware stores to McDonald's and U-Haul. All of them were more approachable, enthusiastic, and generous when presented with targeted theater programs for specialized, underserved audiences in their own communities and service areas.

The Benefits Are Clear

The civic, moral, and artistic answers to "What can we do?" and "Where can we do it?" are clear and undeniable. But who would have thought that the pragmatic reasons for these idealistic efforts might outweigh even the altruistic?

Ultimately, then, the question is not "How can we afford these new directions and dimensions?" but rather "How can we possibly *not* afford them?"

Let us go wherever the people are and seek and find new audiences, patrons, donors, grants, materials, and money to give us wings.

8 | "These Kids Are Our Future"

How One Company's Outreach Effort Brings Teenagers to Theater

STEPHEN PEITHMAN

W here will tomorrow's audiences come from? That's not a question asked at New Jersey's Paper Mill Playhouse. They know.

Since 1989, the company has bused in nearly four thousand high school students for free matinees, sent artists-in-residence to the schools, and given youngsters the opportunity to perform their original plays on the Playhouse stage.

For companies wondering how to replace aging patrons (see Chapter 18, "When Your Audience Ages"), the remarkable Adopt-a-School program and its offshoots offer an object lesson.

The program began nine years ago when the company learned that students at nearby Newark Arts High—one of the oldest performing-arts high schools in the country— weren't going to the theater, mostly because they couldn't afford to.

In response, Paper Mill began inviting groups of forty students to Thursday matinees at its theater in Millburn, New Jersey. By the fall of 1997, nine high schools from across the state were active participants in the program.

Because the students come from racially and economically diverse backgrounds, not all were comfortable at first.

"Some kids came in feeling, 'This is too fancy. We don't belong here,' " says the company's director of education, Susan Speidel.

To help them feel more welcome while teaching them about theater, Paper Mill began offering a special hour-long session before each show. For a recent production of *Big River*, for example, students were shown a model of the set, and how most of the automated set changes worked.

"We explained the rest of the tricks at intermission, after they'd had a chance to see part of the show," Speidel says. "Then the actor who played Huck talked about how someone in his late twenties could play a fourteen-year-old."

Before other shows, the groups may meet with a director, a lighting designer, or a makeup artist who does special effects. For all productions, Speidel sends out study guides "because some shows make more sense when the kids understand the frame of reference. We try to demystify the theater experience for them. We make it clear to them that we want them here, that we're interested in them, that we care about them."

After seeing five shows, students come to see Paper Mill as *their* theater, Speidel says. She's seen many come back as college students to get student-rush tickets or even become subscribers.

"It's become part of their lives," she says, adding that the students also have become part of the life of the theater. Indeed, the student audience has merged with the more traditional audience in ways no one could have predicted. After one show, several youngsters approached Speidel and asked her where "Bob" was.

"I didn't know who they were talking about until they explained that Bob was an elderly man who always sat in front of them at the matinees. They often talked with him, but he wasn't there this time, and they were worried about him."

Residency Outreach

Adopt-a-School has evolved into a three-year program in which most students enter as sophomores and stay until they graduate.

The second year is an artist-in-residency program in which Paper Mill sends creative artists into the schools to help students develop and produce original scripts. Four schools are in this second phase, and the company works closely with teachers at each one, ensuring that the residency complements existing programs.

"I come from a family of educators," Speidel explains. "I admire teachers and supporting their work in the classroom is important to me."

With the residents' help, students write and produce a thirty- to forty-five-minute performance piece, which can be an adaptation or an original work. Each May, students present their work on the Paper Mill stage.

"We do it on a Tuesday night when the theater is otherwise dark," Speidel says. "Students rehearse during the day, then perform that night. Our audiences, our board of trustees attend and students are thrilled to perform on the same stage where they've seen so many of our shows."

In the third and last year of the program, Paper Mill provides master classes in subject areas requested by students, such as makeup or stage combat.

This artist-in-residency program was expanded last year when teachers asked that it include the particular needs of some schools. For example, after a school in Linden renovated its auditorium, it discovered it didn't have anyone who knew how to use all the equipment. Paper Mill is providing a technical director to help the drama teacher learn the new technology.

Another school with a fledgling dance department needed help with a production of *West Side Story*. Paper Mill provided an artist-in-residence to give dance workshops each Friday for three months.

"It was a schoolwide effort," Speidel says. "Even members of the football team expressed an interest and took a beginners' class, with the coach's full support."

Separate from Adopt-a-School is a complementary outreach effort named The Rising Star Awards, a statewide awards program for high school musical productions. Begun in 1996 and modeled on the Tony Awards, Rising Star involves eighty high schools across the state.

More than fifty judges see these schools' musical productions, then submit comments and ratings to Paper Mill, which creates a slate of nominees. The judges return for a day-long meeting, reviewing their comments and looking over photos and other background material sent in by the schools. The winners are selected and in May, Paper Mill hosts a major awards ceremony.

"All the nominated schools send faculty, students, and parents," Speidel says. "Nominees for outstanding actor and actress perform, and production numbers from the top five nominated shows are performed as well. It's a major event and we promote it that way."

Making It Work

Speidel believes the Adopt-a-School program could be duplicated almost anywhere, although she also points out a number of challenges.

"The biggest challenge is scheduling," she says. "You have to schedule a year in advance so you can get on the school calendar. Sometimes a teaching artist has to cancel because of a professional commitment such as a national tour, and you'll have to find a replacement at the last moment. Travel is also a challenge. I and my assistant are on the road two or three days a week."

"We also spend a lot of time talking with our academic partners so we don't duplicate their efforts. And we work hard to get talented artists who also understand how to share their skills in the classroom. That's not always easy."

The concept of a partnership extends to the students as well.

"This is about getting the students involved and taking an active role," Speidel says. "We don't say 'Here is this program we've created and you have no stake in it.' We are always checking to see if we're meeting their needs. I may do an acting seminar for three schools, but if I know students at the fourth are more interested in lighting, I'll tailor that workshop to their interests. You have to be flexible."

All programs except The Rising Star Awards are offered free to schools—underwritten or provided free of cost. The Rising Star Awards program has an entry fee of $35 per school and Paper Mill sells tickets for the awards ceremony, which pays for the event.

Some of the Adopt-a-School costs are borne by the company, Speidel explains, such as setting aside seats for every Thursday matinee. But Paper Mill also has secured funding from corporations and foundations. One of its biggest supporters is Schering-Plough Pharmaceuticals, which told Paper Mill it gets a better, more-rounded employee from those with exposure to the arts, Speidel says.

Outside funding has been particularly important in paying for transportation.

"Many districts don't have buses that can be used for long-distance travel, so we charter buses to bring students here," Speidel explains. "We've worked with the same bus company since 1989. They give us a great price and students like it because it's not a yellow school bus. Of course, just having the buses isn't enough. You need commitment from the schools and the students, and they've come through. For example, because it's in farm country, High Point High School begins at 7:30 A.M. and ends at 2:15 P.M. Our matinee begins at 2 P.M. Some students have to reschedule jobs or give up other activities, but we've never had an empty seat."

The Adopt-a-School program has developed in an almost organic way until, today, it involves twelve groups of students from nine schools. Newark Arts High has been a proving ground for each phase and offers all three phases of the program simultaneously.

"As each phase evolved, it became very apparent what the next step was going to be," Speidel says. "After we had been bringing kids to the theater to see shows, teachers at Arts High came to us and asked if we could give students a chance to perform. That led to Phase Two.

"Phase Three, our workshop and master classes, came out of a comment by a teacher at Rosa Parks High School in Patterson, who told us that we had become its main theater resource. That made us think about bringing in experts for dialect study, advanced makeup, and stage combat to help students work on skills they themselves asked for.

"We've brought in all kinds of expertise to meet those needs. I wouldn't be surprised if someday they ask for a workshop on circus skills," she says with a laugh, "and we'll have to find someone to come in and teach that. It can be an effort," she says, in a more serious tone, "but it's an effort we're willing to make. These kids are our future."

Packing Them in at the Library | 9

TERRI RIOUX

Y our community library offers a place for you to develop a theater audience, and you don't even have to push books aside. Most libraries have a community room with an ample supply of chairs for meetings and presentations. After library hours, this room can become a cozy theater that will draw your audience to play readings that require few if any props.

Tom Holehan is a director who led his community-theater group to the national finals of the American Association of Community Theatre's AACT/Fest competition and to the Great Canadian International Theatre Festival as U.S. representative. He says play readings at his local library helped build an audience that three years later became subscribers to a professional theater company that Holehan and others established in Stratford, Connecticut.

The professional company, Square One Theatre, performs in a renovated movie theater owned by a local civic organization. The theater seats 230 and Square One has 600 subscribers for its current season.

Readers Theatre Showcase, the series of play readings at the Stratford Library that Holehan initiated a decade ago, has offered audiences plays such as *A Walk in the Woods, Steel Magnolias,* and *The Cocktail Hour,* as well as new plays by emerging playwrights. He started the play readings at the library to fill a void in the community left by the vacant American Festival Theatre, to explore new plays opening off-Broadway, and to give playwrights an opportunity to polish their new works. "What more appropriate place to celebrate authors' works than the library?" asks Holehan.

As a community-theater director, you can approach libraries or schools to start your own play-reading performance, too. "A lot of times, organizations in the town are looking for entertainment vehicles or someone to take on projects," says Holehan. Here's how you can set up a series of play readings in your community.

Get Ready

■ *Contact the person responsible for programming* at the library or organization that has rooms available for community use. Discuss your idea, seating capacity, show times, and whether you'll be able to serve refreshments after the show so playwrights, actors, and guests can share their thoughts.

■ *"Always start small and do things perfectly"* when building a theater group and an audience, Holehan says. "Don't try to produce *Oklahoma!* your first year. You've got to be realistic." Start with play readings with two characters with contemporary plays that don't need special costumes. The basic format is a narrator, actors, and a couple of stools.

■ *Pick your plays.* Holehan reads reviews in *Variety* and the *New York Times* to find plays, and favors off-Broadway plays "that take chances." Spread the word among actors and others in the theater community that you're doing play readings. You'll see that new scripts will find their way to you.

The most important criteria for choosing a play is the strength of the dialogue. Don't pick a play that has too much action. Holehan says, "Sex farces don't work. Clothing has to be taken on and off and actors have to be running in and out doors.

"The plays that we usually pick are geared around a specific event or week. The newspapers pick right up on it. If you work in the library, you know every month or week there's a theme." For example: Banned Books Week (*Animal Farm*); AIDS Awareness Month (*On Tidy Endings*); Valentine's Day (*Love Letters*); Christmastime (*Reckless,* a comedy about Christmas); and Women's History Month (*Waiting for the Parade*).

- *Check royalties.* Contact the producing agent about royalties to read a play. The fee varies, says Holehan, but it's usually small for one night's reading.

- *Choose actors.* Having directed another community-theater group for years, Holehan had a resource of actors to choose from for his play readings, but he says he holds open auditions every year. Select actors just as you would for a full production. Holehan says, "I find actors love doing play readings because there's little rehearsal time involved, and they don't have to remember lines, which is the biggest fear that most actors have. So they can relax." (Actors perform with scripts in hand.)

- *Rehearse.* Reading rehearsals are really workshops. If you know your actors, usually one rehearsal will do. As a director, your effort is to bring out the essence of the play and the script. The actual play reading, says Holehan, "runs on sheer adrenaline. It has an energy that sometimes you don't find until opening night."

Get Set

- *Decide if you want to charge admission.* Readers Theatre Showcase is free, but a donation is suggested to cover the cost of refreshments served after the show and most patrons comply. Sometimes donations are requested for charitable organizations. Actors donate their time, talent, and energy.

- *Take reservations*, it will get crowded. Attendance at each Readers Theatre Showcase performance usually fills one hundred seats.

- *Publicize.* Create in-house flyers for the library and get on the library's calendar of events. Send press releases to community publications. Photos help, either headshots of actors or a mock-up scene from your play. "Rather than talking heads, newspapers like different angles on a picture. For *Reckless*, actors were photographed draped in tinsel and lights. For *Steel Magnolias*, actors in animated poses held hair dryers. You can get publicity by timing the play reading to coincide with an event or holiday," says Holehan, "but that doesn't always work."

Go

- *A host/narrator should welcome the audience and introduce the format.* Before the play begins, Holehan explains that play readings are like theatrical radio. Use your imagination, he tells the audience. You're not going to see fancy costumes or props. The narrator stands off to the side and reads from a podium as required by the script.

■ *Encourage feedback.* After the play, the host should encourage the audience to stay for refreshments and to share opinions. You need someone to start the feedback, says Holehan. "People are sometimes reticent, with the actors there, to give their opinions, but I've seen it improve as it goes along. If you really work at it, you get people to say, 'Well, that didn't really work for me,' and then you get a constructive argument going in the audience. It's very important for the playwright to see and hear what's working and what isn't."

Attracting a New Audience | *10*

Community outreach is just the beginning. You've brought the theater to the people; now, how do you bring the people to the theater? Once you've determined who you are, how you are perceived, what audiences you want to attract, and where those audiences can be found, the natural next step is developing specific strategies to attract those audiences. Over the next several chapters, you'll read about particular ways theaters can bring in those customers, beginning with what has now become standard operating procedure for most theaters: turning the single-ticket buyer into a season-ticket holder.

Magic in the Season Ticket?

Michael Kanter

Within the sphere of the theater, selling does not resemble that of any other business. In any business selling a product, a package must be taken off the shelf every time a sale is made. If the item goes out of style, or is preempted by a better, competitive one, there is always a way to salvage some money by running a special sale.

In a theater, however, every empty seat costs as much to produce as every filled seat. You can put $50,000 into a production and if five thousand people see the show, each seat costs $10 plus running costs.

Not more than six percent of the population can be counted as theatergoers. In smaller communities, the percentage is even less. To reach that minuscule percentage of the public who might come to the theater, the cost is mountainous.

If those people who profess to be loyal theatergoers were to simply come to the box office, motivated by modest newspaper announcements, the heavy cost of selling would be reduced, ticket prices would come down, or more money could be spent on the production.

But audiences are unpredictable. All sorts of reasons keep them away from the theater, even if they want to come. All are justifiable obstacles to theater attendance, but a theater must have audiences. Good intentions don't pay bills.

Now the law of probability rears its head. With a subscription roster of seventy to ninety percent of seating capacity, audience attrition can be made up from year to year. With a substantial core audience, a theater can navigate the treacherous shoals of unknown or avant-garde plays. After all, "hits" can never occur without a steady procession of venturesome works. Suppress the production of "misses" and you prevent the "hit" from happening.

A vigorous, artistically valid theater company must reach for new dimensions; that is its responsibility to the community. In return, it has a right to expect its audiences to reciprocate with an expression of confidence and loyalty. A season ticket is that expression.

For many years, the single-ticket route was the staple of noncommercial theaters. It did not work.

The Dallas Theatre Center went from two thousand to almost eleven thousand subscribers via hard-hitting sales campaigns. In just two years, Neptune Theatre of Halifax, Nova Scotia, went from nil to 3,500. In one season, Montreal's Theatre du Nouveau Monde attracted 83,000 members and Theatre Toronto, 11,150.

Until the advent of the subscription concept, noncommercial theaters failed almost universally to develop regular audiences beyond thirty to forty percent of their seating capacity. They would not understand that the money invested in a subscription campaign is not an out-of-pocket expense, but rather a capital investment that comes back through the augmented sale of subscriptions for seats that otherwise would have remained empty, producing not a penny of revenue.

It makes little difference how much is spent to fill seats that would otherwise remain empty. If it costs $8 to sell a $10 seat that would not be filled through normal box-office sales, you are two dollars to the good and six dollars have been paid back. This is fundamental. No other arithmetic applies to the theater.

A capital investment to obtain a large subscription roster carries over into succeeding seasons because most subscribers renew year after year. There's a divorce case on record in which the litigants were more bitter over who would get the season-ticket renewal priorities than they were over the custody of the children!

What does the subscriber get that makes the subscription such a prize? He gets priority-seating locations before seats go on sale at the box office. He gets all his seats without visits to the box office. He owns the same reserved seat for all the plays of the season. He merits preferred seating before seats are put on sale to the public.

There's another valuable aspect to the subscription plan. The once-in-a-while theatergoer who finally takes the plunge into subscriber status is now susceptible to the playgoing habit. Soon he becomes more perceptive, more sensitive to effective writing, skillful stagecraft, and performing virtuosity. His theater horizons are broadened, he gets more for his money, and you have gained a loyal friend.

Because season-ticket subscribers take a more personal interest in the theater as members of the "family," they generate a widening audience by drawing friends and business associates into your orbit. When they can't make the show for one reason or another, they give their tickets to someone who can, and new prospects for subscriptions are born.

The subscription concept has generated new audiences that have, in turn, provided the impetus for the creation of new and better theater organizations all over North America: more theater, more productions, vastly increased audiences, more frequent attendance. And the term *noncommercial* no longer means a lack of production quality.

A revitalized theater of force, depth, vitality, and scope has been launched by the powerful magic of the subscription order blank.

11 | Talking Them into Their Seats

While you concentrate on community outreach and focus on new strategies to attract patrons, it is vitally important that you do not forget the oldest strategy of all: word-of-mouth. It still brings people to the theater, and you have to make sure the word-of-mouth about your productions is good—and circulates as much as possible.

It's Cheap, and It's Effective

MICHAEL E. CAFFERKY

You've been selected to be the producer for the comedy *The Royal Family* and you have about $50 to spend on promotion. How are you going to fill the seats for nine performances?

My answer may surprise you: word-of-mouth. As marketing people will tell you, it's the best advertising there is. Best yet, talk is cheap, and who wouldn't enjoy boasting that a production sold out because of word-of-mouth marketing? The challenge is in knowing how word-of-mouth *really* works and how to encourage customers to talk for you.

Of course, we all talk, but social scientists know that some people are listened to more than others. These are the ones you want to be talking about your theater. Essentially, they are perceived to be believable, genuine, experienced, and interested in what they are talking about. Positive talkers are self-confident and innovative. They have a high degree of social interaction and may be formal or informal leaders in their community.

These champion patrons are interested in live theater and related subjects: they read reviews and scripts and they talk with their friends. Last, and most important, those who have successfully referred customers to you in the past are most likely to continue talking positively about your programs in the future.

You may not be able to apply all these factors equally to all patrons, but make your best judgment and identify, *by name*, the most likely talkers. Don't just think about the customers who have been coming to all your productions for years. Talkers can be new customers too. What you are looking for is leadership—those to whom others listen.

How Leaders Create Success for You

This leadership is the basis of successful word-of-mouth marketing efforts. With their own personal experience as evidence, champion patrons reduce someone else's risk of having a less-than-satisfactory experience. These champions are highly persuasive because they have nothing to gain by their talk.

Consider that a prospective customer may know that your theater exists—they see it listed in the telephone book or in a chamber of commerce directory. But knowing about you isn't enough. What counts is an opinion leader who helps shape their attitude just before making the decision whether to call the box office for tickets.

Practical Ideas to Implement the Theory

1. *Word-of-mouth marketing* begins when you exceed each customer's threshold of positive expectations. Start by building a foundation of excellent productions. Then, have someone help you walk through the whole process (from a new customer's point of view) of searching for information about the theater—from locating you, to ticket-buying, to attending the performance. Where can subtle irritations and frustrations be removed? Where can you add just a touch of class to surprise your patrons and send them home marveling at the great experience they had at the performance?

2. *Follow this protocol* to generate more referrals of new patrons. First, identify your champions by name. Encourage your team to be on the lookout for current customers who meet the selection criteria noted previously. Have a volunteer go through the theater's mailing list and ask veteran company members which names fit the description of opinion leaders. (These veterans should include actors, directors, technical assistants, and other staffers who know the theater from the inside and who are also opinion leaders. With their inside knowledge of your theater, they are also your best

source of new customers.) Next, encourage the champions to talk with their friends and families by keeping them well informed and by asking for referrals. Third, find out from new customers *exactly* who referred them to the show. Fourth, celebrate each referral these champions make for you. If you ignore their efforts, they may stop helping you.

3. *Give more information* to your customers to help them understand the what and why of your theater. Give private showings of short one-act plays where your champions work or get together. This will give them a natural opportunity to talk about community theater and invite their friends for a performance. Make extra sure your champions are well informed about "the goings on" from the inside. The more information the better, and the more from personal experience the better.

4. *Get champions involved* with the program by drawing them into the production planning process. Create a community advisory board from your champion list. Have them sit down with you and discuss their ideas. Get their feedback on your approach to play selection, casting, and other details. Invite them to volunteer in some behind-the-scenes work.

5. *New customers* who are attending for the first time should be given the royal treatment. Make it a point to have your staff speak with these individuals personally before or after the performance. If you wish, you can invite newcomers back stage after the production to meet some of the cast and to survey behind the scenes; while there, they are treated to wine and cheese or some other treat. This is not merely a pleasant social event, but rather your opportunity to hunt for people you meet who match the opinion-leader criteria.

6. *Rewards for referrals* are vital. At the bare minimum, give each referring customer a verbal and written thank-you. At all performances, give verbal public recognition, thanking them "for the positive impact they have had on the theater by sharing with the community experiences they themselves have had. This has resulted in a growth of attendance." If possible, recognize by name specific champions who have brought in new season-ticket holders. This may be done tastefully on a bulletin board in the lobby. Don't be surprised if someone comes to the box-office window and asks why their name is not on the "Hall of Champions" list because they bring guests to the theater all the time. If you can identify a few champions who do exceptional work in referring others to buy tickets, give them something tangible in appreciation—a dinner and gift for their efforts, for example.

7. *Conduct educational programs* for schoolteachers, company activity directors, and church program directors in your area, helping them learn "how to use the power of drama" in their particular setting. Being a leader in the training of others will enhance your credibility as a leader in quality live theater as well. Start with the organizations to which your champions belong.

8. *Have a formal system to deal with complaints.* Sometimes things go wrong for the customers. Someone messes up their reservation. Their tickets get lost. They find gum on their seat five minutes before the show. Some patrons may bring their problems to you. Your complaint-handling system should include the following steps:

a. Acknowledge their frustration or complaint.

b. Tell them that you are glad they brought this to your attention.

c. Get their ideas of what it will take to solve the problem. Make sure the customer understands what is possible and what is not. Then act quickly.

d. Always follow up with customers later to see if the problems have been resolved to their satisfaction.

9. *Plan several weeks in advance* of each production how your champions will bring in the customers. Here's an example of an incentive system to try: Champions who bring in ten or more customers during the performances get a chance at receiving a free pass to all of next season's performances. Engage your staff in calling the champions, telling them about the upcoming production, and asking them for their support in bringing new customers.

10. Finally, *conduct short training classes* for all theater staffers in the fine art of customer relations, including proper etiquette, handling problems, and an awareness of customers' expectations.

12 | Special Productions Can Bring in the Public

One way to increase the size and scope of your audience is to offer special productions once or twice a year. A good example is a yearly holiday production, such as *A Christmas Carol*, which is standard fare in many cities, including Chicago's Goodman Theatre and San Francisco's American Conservatory Theater.

Such productions are not only major moneymakers (reason enough to consider them), but they also have a more important function: They bring in a different audience than that which attends during the regular season, including younger (twenty-five to thirty-five-year-old) patrons and families. This large group of new theatergoers is important to your health, for once they step into your foyer, they know where you are. And if they have a good time, they are more likely to consider coming back.

Use the opportunity for all it's worth. Advertise your season in the lobby and in your program. Have posters and flyers handy—and, more important, a representative in the lobby to hand them out and answer questions. Invite newcomers to add their names to your mailing list, explaining that they'll get advance information for upcoming shows so they can get good seats. Better yet, have tickets on sale for those upcoming shows as well.

If you're lucky enough to own or rent your own theater space, you might consider this idea from the Goodman Theatre. The Goodman presented a local dance company in a concert at the theater. Again, the audience for the dance concert proved to be quite different than that for either the regular season or its Christmas production. Once again, the theater made sure these new audiences heard about the Goodman's offerings and got their names on the mailing list. Eventually, with the help of a corporate sponsor, the Goodman was able to present several companies in a full dance series.

Look around your own artistic neighborhood. If you have your own theater space, consider donating use of it to a local dance company, orchestral ensemble, band, or choral group. Not only is there the possibility that you can turn your generosity into a larger audience for your own productions, but you also can turn it into bountiful PR in the local media—again putting your name before the public.

13 | *New Plays Bring New Audiences*

W hen we speak of "audience development," it's usually in the sense of building the number of people who come to our productions. *Who* these people are (other than labeling them "theatergoers") isn't usually as important as getting them to buy tickets.

However, there is another type of audience development, targeted at very specific audiences. Chicago's Victory Gardens Theater has taken this concept and blended it with artistic development to develop a previously untapped market.

For the past few years, Victory Gardens has presented a "Night of Scenes," a free evening of theater in which three scenes by playwrights of color are presented to an invited audience. The event serves as "an introduction to the theater for people who often have never stepped inside our doors before," according to theater spokesperson Barbara Griffin.

In addition to increasing the theater's African American and Hispanic audience, the "Night of Scenes" program has helped the theater find work by playwrights of color for productions, workshops, and residencies.

Broadening the diversity of its offerings and its audience

is important in Chicago, where Hispanic people account for twenty percent of the city's population. The African American community continues to be an important part of the city's strong mix of cultures and ethnic groups.

The Victory Gardens program not only increases the awareness of these audiences for theater itself, but the company also surveys the audience for feedback on the scenes presented. This offers the company's artistic staff a chance to see which plays are well liked and which scenes the audience feels need further development.

"The playwrights gain greatly from the experience of having professional actors perform their scene and witnessing the audience reacting to their work," says Griffin.

The brainchild of Artistic Associate Jaye Stewart, the event was first presented in 1991. Since then, Victory Gardens has presented many such evenings and the results have been "extremely positive," Griffin says.

For example, *Freefall*, by Charles Smith, was first presented in the "Night of Scenes" program and went on to a mainstage production. The company's twentieth anniversary season presented two plays that were first performed as part of the scenes program: *Real Women Have Curves* by Josefina Lopez and *Get Ready* by Jaye Stewart and Joe Plummer.

In addition to the many actors who have been cast to play the scenes, the program has brought in large numbers of people, with about eleven percent of them becoming Victory Gardens subscribers.

According to Artistic Director Denniz Zacek, the program has proved to be "one of the most vital and practical means of communicating with potential audiences and addressing their needs." The program has been funded by the Lila Wallace–Reader's Digest Resident Theater Initiative. The grant is aimed at increasing the theater's African American and Hispanic audiences.

In the first three years of the program, Griffin says, "the diversity of the theater's subscriber base has increased, as well as the number of artists that the theater is working with. As a theater dedicated specifically to the work of the living playwright, we are encouraged by the increased awareness of theater, the added subscribers, the number of plays presented, and the playwrights that the theater has been able to support."

14 | Off the Beaten Track?

How One Out-of-the-way Theater Pulls Them in by the Busload

LISA LAWMASTER HESS

Your theater company is off the beaten track. You're out in the woods, in the country, away from the hustle, bustle, and population centers where your potential audience congregates. Will anyone come to see a show all the way out here? How will they even know the theater exists? How do you get them to make the long trip out to see you—and how do you keep them coming back?

General Manager Dean Goodwin of the Rainbow Dinner Theatre in Paradise, Pennsylvania, has some answers. His theater is in Lancaster County, famous mostly as home to the Amish, who find themselves regularly invaded by tourists dying to see how people can survive without cars, computers, and cellular phones.

Goodwin has made a virtue out of necessity. Without an immediate population base to draw from, his theater relies on tourists, trucked in by the busload. He's learned how to reach them and he's learned how to cultivate them. The lessons he's learned have value for any company searching for ways to reach an audience.

Getting to Know You

"All I have to do [to get people out here]," says Goodwin simply, "is get everybody to know about us."

Goodwin does that not only through local advertising, but also through frequent contact with many, many tour-group leaders and bus companies. Rainbow is a member of several bus associations and visitors' bureaus, as well as a founding member of C-PATH, the Central Pennsylvania Theatre Association.

Goodwin's mailing list, ten years in the making, numbers more than seven thousand tour-group leaders. It started with cold calls to bus companies and other organizations that had access to groups. In addition, Goodwin has a separate mailing list for individuals who attend some or all of Rainbow's four shows per year, which frequently sell out. An invitation in the program asks patrons if they wish to be included on the company's mailing list.

What do you do with all those names on the mailing list?

"Call, call, call, send, send, send, visit, visit, visit!" Goodwin exhorts. "You call the [tour] group leaders. You send direct mail to the group leaders and the tour operators, and you visit the tour operators and their group-leader shows."

Group-leader shows give restaurants and dinner theaters—known in the trade as *properties*—an opportunity to talk to large numbers of leaders in one fell swoop. Each property rents a booth and stocks it with necessary materials such as brochures, a brag book, and possibly some door prizes, as well as an enthusiastic spokesperson. Shows like these are one of the perks that can make selling to the motorcoach industry easier than soliciting local businesses.

"You have one person who's in charge of forty-six people," says Goodwin. "I only have to sell one person—the group leader or the tour operator. *They* are in charge of going out and selling forty-six seats."

In addition to working with tour operators and group leaders, Goodwin utilizes people called *receptive operators* to get the word out. Receptive operators work much like travel agents, making all arrangements for groups, then quoting a price for the whole package. Receptive operators market only one destination, however, receiving visitors into that area—unlike a travel agent who can send you anywhere.

Rainbow provides receptive operators with its lowest available ticket price as an incentive to send tourists its way. Tour operators also receive a lower price than individuals or nontour groups because they relieve Rainbow of the time and expense required to market to the travelers in their group.

Come Again?

Okay, you've gotten your audience out to see you. Now, how do you keep them coming back?

Goodwin's boundless enthusiasm and genuine concern for Rainbow's patrons are probably among the best tools in his marketing arsenal.

"It has to be everybody's magical day," he enthuses. "Everyone who's coming through is seeing [the show] for the first time."

Group leaders are greeted by name upon their arrival. Staff members are up-to-date on where the group is from, how many times the group has been to Rainbow, and what show they last saw. The producers, David and Cynthia DiSavino, attend every performance (and perform in many as well), and station themselves at the doors to say goodbye and thank you to everyone who attends the show. Groups attending the show are acknowledged at the end of the performance, as are the birthdays and special occasions of audience members.

According to Goodwin, his audience members are appreciative that Rainbow offers an all-inclusive dinner and theater experience "where the food is as good as the show." In designing Rainbow's new theater, which opened in February 1995, the needs of these particular theatergoers were taken into account. Salads arrive only moments after hungry travelers are shown to their seats, and there are two buffet lines to speed service, staffed with servers who can answer any questions guests may have about the food. There are also "state-of-the-art" ladies' rooms with twelve stalls.

"Sometimes the show [title] sells, sometimes the period will sell, but I think you have to give them a quality product, no matter what it is," asserts Goodwin.

Locally, Goodwin understands he must win the loyalties of both theatergoers and restaurant patrons.

"I have to convince the theater people that this is going to be a theater experience, because dinner theater for a very long time has had a kind of negative image, the 'chew and view' attitude," he explains. "And I have to convince the restaurant public they're going to have a superior product too." Rainbow utilizes professionals both in its kitchen and on its stage. Chefs from the nearby Revere Tavern prepare the food for each show and, because Rainbow is a professional company, patrons usually find a mix of local talent and actors from New York and Philadelphia on stage.

Goodwin knows who his patrons are and from where they are coming, so he supplements their word-of-mouth advertising with carefully placed ads of his own. Rainbow advertises weekly in both local newspapers and those in neighboring counties. In addition, Rainbow advertises on local radio stations that serve its target demographic, supplementing those ads with giveaways to keep its name out there when the ads aren't running. As a member of visitors' bureaus in Lancaster County and nearby Valley Forge, Rainbow utilizes their publications to further spread the word.

Last spring, Rainbow worked with three other Lancaster theaters, renting a van to go on a sales blitz. The aim was to market Lancaster as a theater destination. The theaters feel that by working together, each theater can share its strengths and its connections.

Perhaps Rainbow's main strength in attracting and keeping audiences is its attention to personal details. Goodwin himself greets audience members by name, and says that "you always have to be there. You just can't let somebody else do the job who is maybe not as detail-oriented as you are."

Particularly when you're off the beaten track.

15 Committing to the Classics

What to Do if Your Public Isn't Familiar with Once-popular Titles

DIANE CREWS

H ave you ever selected a show that is so well known you thought it would be a sure thing? Maybe a sellout? And then the tickets didn't sell at all?

I have found, much to my chagrin, that "well known" to some of us does not mean the general public or younger theater people know many of what I call modern classics. I think we need to do something about that.

What's happened to us at Pennsylvania's York Little Theatre the last few years illustrates well, I think, why we need to take action.

A few Christmases ago, we needed a fundraiser and so produced what I felt was a perfect holiday show. Our house holds 250. The performance I attended had an audience of about sixty . . . maybe. Later that week, at a play-reading committee meeting, I expressed my disbelief at the public's lack of response. But it turned out that only *one* of eight members of my own committee had ever heard of the show, and none of them had ever seen it.

So a very strong production almost went unseen. The show? *Amahl and the Night Visitors.*

"Everyone" Doesn't Know

Even that experience did not prepare me for what happened next. A special production was switched from our studio space to our main stage because we were certain that audience demand would necessitate the extra seating capacity. The royalties we had to pay were more than double our standard, but so—we felt—was the potential box office. Everyone would want to come to this.

As director, I had been asked to speak at several community functions about the production, and although I didn't think extra publicity was needed, I also knew you can never have too much.

My first stop was a monthly dinner meeting of a local accountants group. At meal's end, while the pianist warmed up, I told the audience how pleased I was to be there and how excited the theater was to be bringing this particular production to the community. I assured them they would recognize immediately the music they were about to hear. Out of curiosity, I asked those who had seen the show somewhere before to raise their hand. Of close to 150 in the audience, there were only three hands in the air!

The show was *The Fantasticks*.

Fortunately, we managed to make enough to cover royalties and expenses, and there are now about one thousand new people in my area who can raise their hand. However, there also were two thousand empty seats.

Self-Fulfilling Prophecy

Wondering whether this was just a local problem, I began surveying other theaters. The same answers kept surfacing: "They will only come if it's just been made into a movie." "People don't know these titles." "The old shows are too long." "They're dated." And so on.

Well, at least we've identified a problem that we can do something about. It seems to me that it is *our* fault people don't know these titles—and it's us who can change things.

It's the ultimate self-fulfilling prophecy. By not doing our own classics, we cut off the most obvious avenue for their continuance in the hearts and minds of the public.

Do you remember the first time you saw *Our Town* or *The Glass Menagerie* or *The Crucible*? Do you go to see other productions of these plays when they are nearby? I do, and I know why: It's because I remember them. I have experienced them somewhere along the line, and I was hooked.

I'm not suggesting a whole season of oldies. I'd settle for one per season and a commitment to a revival of that title every ten to fifteen years. But, of course, just doing them is not sufficient to ensure their survival either. We must do them well. Nothing can beat a good production of a great play. And we must advertise what to many has become an unknown title.

How? Find an angle, whether it be nostalgia or the universality and timeliness of a classic. Or do what a local high school did here recently. The headline on one of its flyers read, "We Beat Broadway." They were mounting a production of *How to Succeed in Business Without Really Trying*, and their production ran a week earlier than when the Broadway revival began its run.

Making a Commitment

The Lancaster Opera Workshop in Pennsylvania did its first production of *Amahl and the Night Visitors* some forty-five years ago. The show was new then, and being shown every Christmas on television, so the audiences were excellent. But as years went by, interest waned and people began to forget the story and lose interest.

What did the Opera Workshop do? Stop mounting the production and never do it again? No, they made a commitment to a classic and continued *Amahl* as an annual event. The group ultimately chose to take the production on the road, and they now have a beautifully mounted touring show that goes into churches, schools, and other theaters. The demand is so great, they take bookings a year in advance. The audience has experienced *Amahl* and it has become part of its Christmas.

(Such a happening is not uncommon. *The Nutcracker*, that beloved classic ballet, was practically unknown in this country until television reintroduced it to America in the 1950s. Now it's a holiday standard.)

Like the folks involved with that *Amahl* production, I fervently believe: If we do the classics, the audience will come, and come, and come again. The proof is in the (Christmas) pudding.

Community Audience for High School Theater | 16

"*How* do we build a community audience for our high school theater?" is a question we've been asked by more than one reader. Actually, the answer isn't much different for *any* theater company. If you want people to come to your productions, offer them something they want to see.

Too often, high school directors think, "The community *ought* to support us," as if there were some sort of general obligation due. It is true that your student actors deserve an audience, but ask yourself why someone would *want* to come to your shows. In other words, don't ask what's in it for you. What's in it for *them*?

Consider the various ways people could spend a Saturday night, for example. They could go to the movies, a sporting event, or a rock concert. They could rent a video and stay home, or just watch television. Or sleep. Or see your play. Whichever, the main driving force is simple: How can I enjoy myself the most with the least amount of effort? Or, if there is effort involved, is the entertainment I receive worth it?

What can you offer that can come close to meeting those needs?

Does It Make Sense?

Before we get on with suggesting ways to attract a community audience, let's pause a moment. Is such an audience a good idea? Are your actors, designers, and technicians ready to be judged by a community audience? Classmates, teachers, and family members have a personal connection to the production. For the most part, the community at large does not.

An outside audience may be more critical, more difficult to please. Ticket-buyers may come expecting production values you can't deliver. They may be disappointed that your version of *West Side Story* or *The Odd Couple* doesn't match the impact of the film or television version.

Then there is the question of reviews. If you seek a community audience, your local newspaper should be able to review your productions as they would with any other theater group. How will a negative review affect your cast and crew? Some papers, we know, soft-pedal the negatives, even to the point of publishing a nonreview. However, the public soon grows wise to such tactics. How would that affect the general perception of your productions?

The strength of a high school theater, it seems to us, is that it gives students a chance to learn without most of the pressures that surround other forms of theater. A director can cast more freely, using people with more potential than polish. Likewise, set and lighting designers have the opportunity to learn as they work.

If audience-building becomes too strong a motive, you may find yourself producing plays with audience popularity in mind. This begins to dictate content, and you may find that while you would *like* your students to have experience with Shakespeare or Moliere, the demands of filling your theater work against that.

And because community audiences may be less likely to forgive shaky acting or technical skills, you may be tempted to use only the strongest actors. If you do, how are the others ever to have the chance to develop those same skills?

How's the Venue?

Let's assume that at this point you still feel comfortable with developing a community audience. Start with a consideration of the physical attributes of your theater space. An audience wants to be comfortable, and it wants to hear what's going on on stage. How comfortable is your theater? How are the acoustics? If you have a well-equipped stage and comfortable seating, you are in good shape. If you stage plays in a multipurpose room or gym, you face an uphill battle in attracting a broader audience. Ask yourself if you would really want to attend a play if you had to strain to hear dialogue or sit on rock-hard seats.

If you have a problem of this sort and you aren't likely to get a new theater in the near future, there may be some Band-Aid solutions. If your audience must sit on metal or wooden folding chairs, offer seat cushions for rent in the lobby and publicize the fact that you do so. Stadium cushions can be purchased inexpensively through a discount sporting-goods store. You'll pay for them after only a few rentals. (If you're worried about people taking the cushions with them, you always can charge a deposit.)

If acoustics are the problem, give some thought to a good sound system. Yes, it can be expensive, but it's a lot cheaper than a new theater. A good system should not overpower the listener or even call attention to itself. The mistake most theaters make is installing one pair of speakers near the proscenium; the volume then has to be cranked up enough for the people in the back row to hear. Instead, put in a pair of small speakers in front and another in the back, and use just enough volume to make dialogue clear.

What Type of Show?

Shows with the greatest name recognition bring in more people than lesser-known shows. That's true for any theater. If you want to increase the size of your audience from the community, you'll have to give more consideration to producing such plays. However, the most popular plays also tend to be the most expensive to produce; royalties usually are higher, and production values may increase the cost as well. You'll need to weigh this as you set your season.

Captive Audiences First

As you promote your productions, your first target should be students, staff, and parents. These people have the most reason to see your shows and the most reason to be proud of your production. Ask yourself if you're doing everything possible to get the word out to these people and to help them understand why they will like what they see.

One trick that isn't used often in this venue is group rates. Why not encourage students or parents to put together a theater group of ten or more to take advantage of a special discount? You also might work out a deal with a local restaurant to offer dinner and a show for a special price.

How about a special mailing to all parents? It needn't be expensively produced. If the school has a nonprofit bulk-mail permit (it can get one if it doesn't), postage for a single-page flyer will cost only a fraction of a first-class piece.

Spreading the Word

Moving out into the community, make use of service groups such as Rotary or Soroptimists. Ask if you can bring some of your performers to a lunch meeting and do a scene or number from the show. Leave a flyer for each member. Better yet, sell tickets while you're there (be sure to let them know ahead of time that you'll have tickets available so they bring cash or checkbooks).

Most churches are happy to encourage students in theater because it provides a healthy spare-time activity. Ask ministers in your area to display posters or perhaps announce the play at the end of services. Find out which students belong to which churches or synagogues, so this can be mentioned in newsletters.

You already may have approached local businesses about putting up a poster in a store or office window. But have you thought of offering two free tickets in return? This is a fine way to get merchants involved and to spread the word to others.

Speaking of merchants, contact your local chambers of commerce—you may find much support there as well. Many chambers stock information on community services and local groups and make this information available to newcomers. Make sure information on your upcoming show is there too.

In the End

All these ideas can help encourage the community at large to attend your productions. However, you haven't really *built* an audience until they keep coming back. Give audiences an enjoyable experience and they will return.

"The Pay's the Thing" | 17

I f you live in an area where there are a number of theater companies, you might want to consider talking to your local newspaper about running an article such as the one we saw in the *Sacramento Bee*. Called "The Pay's the Thing," this nearly full-page article lists ten ways in which readers can save money at area theater companies, including season tickets, group discounts, student and senior discounts, weekday performances, preview performances, pay-what-you-can nights, day-of-performance discounts, discount coupons, dinner theater, and volunteering.

The first five are probably obvious, the second five may need some explanation.

A few Sacramento-area theaters offer one performance per production where audience members pay whatever their budget will bear. At the Foothill Theatre Company, it's the last Thursday of every show's run. At the B Street Theatre, for instance, it's the first Thursday after a show opens. The Sacramento Theatre Company also offers such a performance, but the date varies with each show. STC also offers what it calls a "Hot Tix" deal. Come to the box office between noon and 1 P.M. on the day of the performance and you can buy a ticket at half price.

Miriam Gray's Acting Studio, which presents three or four performances a year, charges $12 for general admission. However, it also sells coupon books, each good for five admissions. Purchasers can use their coupons all at one show or spread them out over several productions. A coupon book costs $30, a fifty-percent savings over single admissions. Many other theater companies accept coupons from discount travel, entertainment, and dining directories—typically two admissions for the price of one.

And dinner theater? The *Bee* article points out that it is both a time- and money-saver. "Instead of going to a restaurant for dinner and then driving to a theater for a play, you can stay in one place and have both, often for less money." Garbeau's dinner theater, for example, charges $26 to $32 for both dinner and a show.

The article ran on the first page of one of the newspaper's Sunday sections, with a list of phone numbers for area theater companies on another page. Such an article in your own local paper is more than a benefit to the theaters—it's a service to the newspaper's readers. Point this out when you raise the idea with your local editor.

When Your Audience Ages | *18*

Perhaps the most significant audience problem facing theaters of all kinds, throughout the country, is the question of aging patrons. It's not exactly a hidden problem. Just look around you the next time you're sitting in the audience: It's likely most of the people you see will be in their forties, fifties, and beyond. These generations reached maturity when theater-going was an integral part of any cultured person's life, growing up when theater going was a regular habit for many and television was not yet on the scene, or new and limited. These generations were contemporary with Rodgers and Hammerstein, Tennessee Williams and Arthur Miller, Lerner and Loewe. They come to the theater now because they came to the theater then. But these audiences are beginning to age out of regular attendance.

In many cases, they are not being replaced by younger patrons. For many younger people, theater has never been an essential part of their life. They don't have the habit. Weaned on Star Wars *and MTV, many believe that theater is too staid, old-fashioned, formal, expensive, and removed from their life. Not without some reason, they believe theater is for older people.*

What to do about the aging problem? Here are some answers.

If You're Fighting the "Blue-Hair Blues," Here's Advice on How to Attract Younger Audiences

STEPHEN PEITHMAN

It's a fact: Theater audiences are aging. According to a recent report by the National Endowment for the Arts (see "Age-Old Questions," Chapter 19), arts attendance has declined along generational lines due to a "massive shift in taste and tradition" as pop music and mass culture displace the traditional performing arts.

This shift, while not uniform in all areas of the country, even has taken on a name: "Blue-Hair Syndrome." We've heard about it from many readers and at many theater conferences: Our audiences are literally dying off, goes the lament. How do we replace them?

No one is suggesting, of course, that there is something intrinsically wrong with older audiences—or blue-tinted hair rinse, for that matter. Rather, the concern reflects the awareness that if theater is to thrive, it must keep current audiences while pulling in younger patrons in increasing numbers.

How do we replace aging audiences? We asked that question of performing-arts organizations around the country. What are they doing to broaden their audience appeal? Here's what we found.

Working with Schools

Bringing plays to the schools introduces youngsters to live theater and thus makes an important long-term contribution. However, a program that brings students *to* the theater has greater potential for audience development. Why? Because young people see a play in a fully equipped theater—your theater. Because it's often their first experience, their excitement and enthusiasm generates positive word-of-mouth about you. Their parents and teachers become familiar with you as well, including where you're located. Bringing the student to the play helps build the theatergoing habit.

That's why North Carolina's Asheville Community Theatre offers morning matinees to area high and junior high schools in February and April. ACT staff members provide teachers with study packets for use in the classroom prior to performance. ACT's offerings are not typical student fare either, but rather plays such as *All My Sons* and *Marvin's Room*. Student admission for the daytime matinees is $4, with free admission for teachers and chaperones.

The Caldwell Theatre Company in Boca Raton, Florida, has run a Theater for Schools program since 1987. Theater for Schools productions are performed without charge on weekday mornings each fall. After the performance, students participate in a question-and-answer period with the actors and production staff. (Caldwell actively solicits corporate and individual donors for the program.)

Special Youth Programs

There is a growing interest in efforts outside the classroom, actively involving young people in productions.

"Our theater has always been a welcoming place for kids who don't do sports," explains Pat Kight of Oregon's Albany Civic Theater. "Drama teachers at both our local high schools feed their kids into our program, particularly the ones who are having trouble with motivation. They often start out working back stage, and we're not afraid to give them responsibility. We've had a thirteen-year-old running lights—and quite well, I might add. A recent assistant director was sixteen and so competent, she's scary. They bring in their friends too."

Recently, the company has begun to offer tuition-based acting and stagecraft classes for elementary and secondary school students. Results have been good not only for the schools, but also for the theater company.

"Many of those kids have begun bringing their parents to see their shows," Kight reports. "Many of those parents will return on their own for our other productions."

Another theater company that gets youngsters involved is Connecticut's Crystal Opera, which offers a youth opera program.

"Children, mostly teens, are introduced to opera," explains David Zack, associate director at the opera. "They perform, they tech, they sing in the choruses of major operas, and even produce student operas. This is the best way I've seen of introducing the next generation to the performing arts, and it also brings their parents to see the shows."

The director holds discussions during which the youngsters deal with the history of the opera, the composer, the production, the context, and the period of the piece. The company's guest artists are invited to participate, and most are willing and eager to do so.

"The kids are encouraged to do additional research," Zack reports, "and, boy, do they! Every year we attract more kids and every year they are younger."

Out of the Rut

Working with young people is an investment in your company's future. So is broadening the audience base to include young adults, particularly those twenty-five to forty years old.

Pat Kight of Albany Civic Theater reports that when she first began working with the company, "the audience pretty much fit the blue-hair cliche—lots of loyal, longtime patrons who were getting old enough that they packed the matinees because they don't much want to go out at night. We used to have Thursday-night shows where there were more people on the stage than in the house."

Such a situation leads to stagnation in many cases. As Douglas Langworthy notes in an article in *American Theatre*, "the harsher economic climate for the arts has caused theaters to become more reliant than ever on box-office income and hence on audiences. A theater's need to hold onto the audience at all costs—afraid of alienating anyone—can amount to a form of self-censorship, preventing it from making risky or demanding choices."

The Albany theater, however, began doing newer, more challenging plays, and making some effort to market them to new audiences—the nearby university community, for instance.

"We do nine to ten productions each season," Kight explains, "so there's still plenty of room for old standards. But what surprised us is that our older patrons turn out for the unusual stuff too. I'm not saying we're wildly avant-garde, but we do try to stretch ourselves—and our audiences—a little. We run in the black, by the way, with no government or grant support. In a town of thirty-two thousand people, we're filling ten to eleven thousand patron seats a year in a 160-seat house."

What the Oregon group discovered is mirrored in the research of Bob Johnson, a graduate student at the University of Maryland, who found that to attract younger adults, a company must start with the selection process.

"Young adults want to attend plays that have name recognition," he says. "Something that has been a pretty popular movie, for example, has a better chance at getting those younger audiences into the theater. If they don't know the play, they want to know what it is about. A focus group I conducted asked for synopses—similar to those that appear on the back of video boxes—to be included on posters and other promotional material."

Other Strategies

David Hansen, who is twenty-seven, was brought to Dobama Theatre in Cleveland Heights, Ohio, in order, he says, "to get a new audience in the seats. Dobama Theater has a reputation for producing the newest plays by established and emerging playwrights and its productions are professionally executed. However, its audience is, for the most part, the same people who started with it thirty-five years ago. Artistic Director Joyce Casey wanted to turn things around."

Hansen created a late-evening series called Dobama's Night Kitchen, whose mission is "to produce original works by today's younger artists that are socially relevant, entertaining to experience, and inexpensive to produce and attend," he explains. Curtain time is 11 P.M. following Friday- and Saturday-night mainstage performances.

The first production was *Bummer*, an original work detailing the real-life traumas of growing up in Cleveland during the late seventies and early eighties. The production was cowritten by an ensemble of young artists under Hansen's direction. This was followed by two editions of *The Realistic World*, a self-titled "experiment in improvisation."

Dobama's Night Kitchen also produced two one-acts, one by George Bernard Shaw, the second a new play by Sarah Morton—two "complementary pieces pertaining to public funding for the arts," Hansen says. All Night Kitchen performances cost $6 or less to attend, and none are more than ninety minutes in length.

Imagination and a good dose of marketing savvy can make a difference. In Allentown, Pennsylvania, for example, The Theatre Outlet offers a series called "Counter Culture" on Mondays, in which different forms of staged productions are performed in a cafe-type atmosphere. Admission is usually around $5 and attracts high school and college students and young adults.

Lower prices are a must if a theater is to attract younger audiences, particularly families. A family of four or five will have a hard time going to the theater if tickets cost $15 to $25 each. And young people, without much experience in theatergoing, are not likely to experiment if the price is high. Thus, many companies offer lower prices for at least one performance, as well as pay-what-you-can nights, "two-fers" (two tickets for the price of one), and student rush (half-price tickets fifteen minutes before curtain). All these are excellent options to keep theater affordable to younger audiences, thus building the theatergoing habit.

And because the price of hiring a babysitter is enough to deter some parents, some theaters are now offering on-site daycare during performances. Center Stage in Baltimore, for example, offers a series called "Child's Play," which provides play-related activities for two- to ten-year-olds while their parents see the show.

Ideas like this and the others we've reported here are only the tip of the iceberg. Every theater company should examine its own efforts to encourage new audiences—everything from examining play selection to changing curtain times. After all, the future of theater is what we make it.

Age-Old Questions | 19

A study commissioned by the National Endowment for the Arts, based on interviews with ten thousand American adults, offers much to chew on. In "Age and Arts Participation with a Focus on the Baby Boom Cohort: 1982–1992," coauthor Judith H. Balfe reports that she found "many simply with no interest in the arts, others with real hostility to them."

An earlier NEA report singled out educational level as the most important variable affecting participation in the arts. The new report argues that this isn't true of younger people and educated baby boomers and suggests instead that education itself has changed. The decline in public-school arts education is representative of a more general problem that will continue to affect society in the years to come.

An article by Edward Rothstein in the *New York Times*, however, points out that while concert halls and theaters are facing problems, art museums are booming. "This may be due in part to our culture's increasing emphasis on the visual, its preoccupation with imagery on television and in movies," Rothstein suggests. "Museums may also demand a lower commitment of money and time than a concert or theater, involve less planning, and require little if any risk of being imprisoned in unpleasantness. They have showed marketing savvy, creating audio tours, gift shops, restaurants, and blockbuster shows."

In "Theatre at the Crossroads," an article in *American Theatre*, writer Douglas Langworthy notes that "many of the structures of institutional theaters—subscription plans, increasing ticket prices, even programming—can discourage nontraditional audiences from attending."

Basing his comments on interviews with more than seventy theater professionals around the country, Langworthy points out that the subscription system in particular has become one of the most problematic aspects of institutional theaters. While it was created to develop a committed ongoing audience that would provide a solid financial base, "subscription may in fact be discouraging the new audiences theaters seek to attract, who find the cost prohibitive and the need to plan months in advance off-putting."

Finally, as we have noted ourselves, theaters must "recommit to cultivating and educating young audiences." That's why, Langworthy points out, many theaters are responding by "intensifying efforts to bring school classes into the theater and by giving higher priority to bringing theater out into the community through youth-oriented outreach programs."

Pay Attention to the Age Wave | 20

You've read and heard about the aging trend in this country, but have you given thought to what this means to your theater company? According to the book, *Age Wave: The Challenges and Opportunities of an Aging America*, by Ken Dychtwald and Joe Flower (Jeffrey Tarcher, Inc.), marketers must consider the following trends:

- The over-sixty-five population has multiplied three times as fast as the population as a whole.

- The number of Americans over sixty-five continues to grow by about a half-million each year. The implications are enormous. The United States is changing, the authors point out, "from a youth-oriented culture into a nation of middle-aged and older adults," and "the effects of every aspect of society will be profound and enduring." Dychtwald and Flower point out that older people are "more interested in purchasing 'experiences' than things." They seek satisfaction, personal well-being, and self-fulfillment. And they have the money to indulge those desires. Mature people consider convenience and access just as important as the product itself. What does this mean to your theater company?

First, take a good look at your audience and your potential audience—that is, the community at large. Are you attracting mature people in numbers equal to their percentage of the local population? If you aren't, consider ways in which you can. Take a look at your season. Are you producing a good mix of subject matter and genre? Mature audiences are conservative, and while you need to allow for variety and artistic breadth, don't overlook a few sure-fire audience-pleasers—they may bankroll that experimental drama or little-known classic.

Check your theater itself. Is your entrance convenient and well lighted? Are aisles easy to negotiate and is there sufficient lighting on them when house lights are down? Are restrooms convenient and well marked? Is the lobby well maintained and large enough to stand without being pushed? You may not be able to remodel your space, but you can put up better signage and make sure ushers are always at the ready with a flashlight during the performance.

Older people often prefer not to drive at night. If your theater is located in the country or in an industrial or inner-city area, experiment with matinees on Saturday and Sunday, and advertise them widely. Offer group rates to senior groups for these performances. Group rates are a good idea at any time. Many senior groups can provide bus transportation for such outings. Another possibility is for your theater company to arrange an evening out: transportation, dinner, and a show. It is hard work, but it can fill the house and get you good publicity in the local media.

Much Ado About Shakespeare | 21

While our theaters may be in competition with other performing arts, as well as with other leisure activities, we don't necessarily have to be competing for an audience with other theaters, too. In fact, some of the most effective ways to attract an audience can be through alliances with other theater companies. In numbers, there can be strength.

Cooperation, Not Competition, Was Their Key to Success

There are few things we at *Stage Directions* find more satisfying than cooperative programs that link theater companies in an effort to share resources and encourage more community participation. The "Seemore Shakespeare" campaign, run by theaters in the Akron-Canton, Ohio, area, is a classic example.

It all began in the fall of 1993. Neil Thackaberry, executive director of the Weathervane Community Playhouse, and David Colwell, managing director of the Porthouse Theatre Company, were talking about various potential cooperative promotional ideas.

"We decided to explore some of these ideas further over lunch," Colwell recalls, "and we invited several other arts administrators from other local theatrical institutions, including Stan Hywet Hall, the University of Akron, and The Players Guild."

The Promotion

From that luncheon came the decision to hold an informal media reception at which the group would announce a cooperative

"Seemore Shakespeare" promotion. The joint program included the following: (1) a direct-mail campaign to ten thousand households using joint mailing lists; (2) special advertising in the playbills of the participating theaters; (3) a special ticket-discount offer; and (4) a bookmark distributed to libraries, bookstores, and other places.

The bookmark idea shows what can be done in a cooperative venture.

"Lisa Alter, general manager of The Players Guild, arranged the printing of the bookmarks at no cost by having them printed on the wasted trim around another brochure she had in production at the time," Colwell explains. "Each participating theater company distributed several thousand bookmarks to bookstores, schools, and libraries in our respective neighborhoods."

Five Shakespeare productions were first considered, but by the time of the media reception in January 1994, the number had grown to six. The first five were *Julius Caesar* (Weathervane Community Playhouse), *Romeo and Juliet* (Players Guild of Canton), *Measure for Measure* (University of Akron), *Henry IV, Part I* (Stan Hywet Shakespeare), and *Much Ado About Nothing* (Porthouse Theatre Company). (Later, the planned production of *Henry IV* was changed to *The Taming of the Shrew*.)

After the reception invitations were mailed, a reporter in Alliance, Ohio, called to see whether the town's Mount Union College had been approached about the promotion.

"When the reporter learned we weren't aware of the college's planned production of *Twelfth Night*," Colwell says, "he called Doug Hendel, director of the production, who in turn contacted us the morning of the reception. We invited him to join the venture, and so that day there were six theaters represented. We highlighted the addition to the media as a concrete demonstration of the effectiveness and power of cooperative ventures of this type."

Winning Media Support

At the reception, the theater representatives announced details of the special discount offer—$2 off each ticket to one Shakespeare production when a ticket stub from any other participating Shakespeare production was presented at the box office.

"We also announced our collective statement of purpose," Colwell says: " 'We hope to raise the visibility of our institutions and to promote the enjoyment of Shakespeare in performance, and build a foundation for future cooperative ventures that will benefit the cultural life of our communities.' " A news release entitled, "Cooperation, Not

Competition, Is the Key to the Future of the Arts," was distributed to the media people who attended and mailed to those who did not.

A one-page article in the Akron *Beacon Journal* with two photographs reported on the Seemore Shakespeare venture. "Our Seemore Shakespeare promotion received further media coverage as well, particularly in the *Beacon Journal*," Colwell reports. "On March 11, 1994, we were featured in the paper's weekly entertainment section. The front page used a color photograph from Weathervane's *Julius Caesar* with the caption, 'It's Hard to Beat the Bard: Local Stages Prove Shakespeare's Staying Power.' Inside was a two-page article that included three photographs. Furthermore, on the front page of the main section was a banner with a small color photograph, with the heading, 'Area Big on Bard: Three Community Theaters Show Shakespeare's Plays. At Least Three More to Come.' "

In addition, Lisa Alter of The Players Guild arranged for an interview between local public-radio station WKSU-FM and her artistic director, Rick Lombardo, who also directed *Romeo and Juliet*.

"This interview was a direct result of the Seemore Shakespeare news release," Colwell says. "Ultimately, WKSU put together a three-minute news piece about *Romeo and Juliet*, as well as the Seemore Shakespeare promotion. It aired three times while that production was in performance. The Players Guild also got several *Romeo and Juliet* sound bites on WKSU during the run. Lisa is certain that the opportunity would not have materialized without the promotion. Their production of *Romeo and Juliet* was a blockbuster hit for them, something they had not originally anticipated."

Pleasing Results

Originally planned for one season, the promotion was "informally prolonged into the 1994–95 season for three of the participants," Colwell says. "Weathervane, The Players Guild, and Theatre Kent extended the Seemore Shakespeare offer by honoring the $2-off discount when patrons brought their stubs from any of the other participating productions to the box office. In addition, each theater ran the revised Seemore Shakespeare ad in their playbills. With the additional three productions added, the promotion was extended an additional seven months, through March 1995."

The added productions were *A Midsummer Night's Dream* (Weathervane Community Playhouse), *Twelfth Night* (Players Guild of Canton), and *Romeo and Juliet* (Theatre Kent at Kent State University).

Among the seven organizations that took part in the promotion, about one hundred ticket stubs were redeemed at the various box offices. "Most of those represented a ticket purchase for at least two people," Colwell says, "so we feel relatively safe in projecting that at least two hundred people crossed over and tried out a second Shakespeare production at a different theater."

The only difficulty surfaced at the Stan Hywet Shakespeare Company, which has no walk-up ticket window for purchasing tickets in advance, Colwell explains.

"Their reservations are done by telephone, supplemented by walk-up sales prior to curtain. For phone orders, ticket verification was not possible. Also, many patrons would reserve tickets but not mention the ticket-stub discount until they showed up at the theater on performance day, ticket stub in hand, to pick up and pay for their tickets. This caused some accounting problems."

In general, however, the participating organizations are pleased with the result of the joint promotion.

"We all agree that, collectively, we generated much more press coverage for our individual shows because of the Seemore Shakespeare promotion angle than we would have otherwise," Colwell says.

The unanticipated success of *Romeo and Juliet* prompted The Players Guild to include *Twelfth Night* in its their subsequent season, he reports. Both Weathervane productions, *Julius Caesar* and *A Midsummer Night's Dream*, enjoyed exceptionally good box office. The University of Akron's *Measure for Measure* played to packed houses. *Romeo and Juliet* at KSU's Theatre Kent enjoyed an exceptional three-week run in its 190-seat Wright-Curtis Theatre.

The latter production "grossed nearly sixteen percent more than its nearest box-office competitor in that theater during the 1991–95 period (*The Importance of Being Earnest*)," Colwell reports. "The production also outstripped other Theatre Kent Shakespearean presentations during that same time frame by thirteen percent of capacity. *Romeo and Juliet* played to ninety-seven-percent capacity; its nearest rival was that theater's production of *The Tempest*, which in 1992 played to eighty-four-percent capacity."

Mulling over the results, Colwell emphasizes that "the administrators of each participating theater feel that the promotion's success can best be measured in terms of increased community and audience awareness of our individual theaters and programs, increased media attention, and increased communication, cooperation, and camaraderie among the theaters and their administrators."

In other words, everyone came out a winner—the companies, their audiences, and the community at large.

Free Discussions Connect Audiences | 22

Whether or not you are part of a theater alliance, we think you will find inspiration in this interesting approach that links a group of local theaters and theatergoers in an informal way.

How Forging Strong Links Can Help Attract Patrons

The New Jersey Theatre Group sponsors a seven-month-long free symposium series called "Talking Stages," focusing on the issues that have inspired plays presented by various member theaters.

While the individual programs are related to specific plays on New Jersey's professional stages, symposium audiences are not required to attend performances. The consortium provides a free printed schedule of the entire symposium series, made possible by a grant from the Prudential Foundation.

The first symposium in a recent year was "From Stage to Screen" at the American Stage Company in Teaneck. A panel of authors and actors who have participated in transfers of stage plays to the screen followed ASC's production of Herb Gardner's *A Thousand Clowns*.

New-play enthusiasts got equal time with a symposium entitled "Looking to the Year 2000" at the McCarter Theatre in Princeton. Writers involved in the theater's month-long new-play festival, "Winter Tales," discussed their craft and the future of drama.

Another symposium was "Myths About Madness: Images of Mental Illness in Art and Popular Culture," at the George

Street Playhouse in New Brunswick. The panel discussion took its cue from Elizabeth Hansen's world-premiere play *Tangent*, which deals with a young person beset by multiple personalities.

A tribute to Martin Luther King, Jr. was a natural for a late-January symposium presented by the Newark Ensemble Theatre. The program came just before performances of *Roads of the Mountaintop*, a new play that examines King's life.

This group promotion benefits all the theaters, providing added value to the theater experience itself. By making this a collaborative effort, individual theaters spread the word about their productions over a wider geographical area as well. You might want to consider doing something like this in your own community. Even if yours is the only community theater, you might join with a local high school or college to provide the same sort of presentations.

Even if a school is not part of the presenting group, make sure you market the presentations to local educational institutions. They should find the symposiums valuable for their students.

Getting the Audience: Did You Know? | 23

*T*he "Did You Know?" department has been a promi-
nent feature of *Stage Directions* since the magazine's
very first issue in 1988. Short items about sundry
theatrical subjects gleaned from companies across
America, various readings, conversations, and other sources,
"Did You Know?" offers an assortment of perspectives. Here
are some hints and pieces of advice on how to attract an audience culled from more than ten years of "Did You Know?"

Come to the Gallery, Stay for the Show

Here's a good way to encourage new audiences while lending
support to the arts in your area. The Croswell Opera House in
Adrian, Michigan, has an art gallery adjacent to the theater that
remains open before performances and during intermission.
Students from the art department of a local high school recently
established their work in the gallery as part of their course re-
quirements for college credit. Not only does the theater audience
provide these students with more exposure, but it also provides
the opera house with community goodwill. We also suspect that
many parents of artists would attend a play, perhaps with

friends, to show off their youngster's talent in the presence of a large audience.

Added Attraction

If you sell season tickets, consider offering subscribers a discount on additional single tickets purchased for friends (based on availability). This is an excellent way to broaden your audience, because newcomers are more likely to attend a production when accompanied by someone who knows and likes what you're doing. When notifying patrons of this service, you may need to include a statement such as, "Because of assigned seating, it may not be possible to seat guests next to their friends."

Reaching Out

Here's a way to bring in audiences that might not be part of your regulars—in this case, Hispanic people in your area. In celebration of *el Diez y Seis de Septiembre*, Adrian, Michigan's Croswell Opera House Minority Advisory Committee and the local Hispanic Heritage Committee presented a Hispanic Heritage Talent Show at the theater. Admission to the show was free; however, donations of $2 per person or $5 per family were requested at the door. Funds collected were used by the two committees to preserve the arts of culturally diverse groups in the area, as well as for a scholarship fund. Besides showcasing the talents of Hispanic members of the community, this event builds goodwill and potential audiences.

The Youth Market

When Arena Stage in Washington, DC, realized it was not attracting young people to its subscriber lists, it revamped its sales procedures to allow young people (who dislike buying advance tickets by mail) to phone in for seats, often at the last minute. The plan worked: Now eighty percent of Arena's single tickets are sold by phone.

Families That Play Together

Studies show that teenagers and the adults they live with spend very little time together. The kids have busy schedules, their parents are absorbed by jobs, and the lines of communication between the two are often tenuous. In an attempt to bring parents and children together, Wisconsin's Madison Repertory Theatre has inaugurated Target Family Night at the Rep for three shows each season. With a grant from Target Stores, the Rep's new program enables high school students and their parents or guardians to attend a play together at no charge. The tickets, which are for preview performances, are distributed through community agencies.

Marketing to the Disabled

A simple way to increase your audience? Market to people with disabilities. How do you do that? Sandra Hartleib, of Very Special Arts Indiana, offers several tips for successful marketing to individuals with disabilities. First, she says, be sure to include information about your facility's physical accessibility and its accessible programming in your overall marketing strategy. Accessibility information should be noted on all brochures, ads, ticket order forms, and press releases.

Also, says Hartleib, note accessibility services by using the universal symbols, because symbols always work better than text. For ticket orders and subscription forms, indicate if wheelchair accessible or nonstep seating is available. Include a floor plan and designate these areas with the universal access symbol.

And, says Hartleib, be sure to use words with dignity to describe people with disabilities. Put people first, not the disability.

On Target

Here's an idea that could be adapted to theater groups. The Saint Paul Chamber Orchestra often targets a particular geographic area and finds a local group to sponsor a performance by the orchestra. There is no charge to the sponsoring group for the orchestra and the group can sell tickets as they please. However, in return for the free performance, the group must provide the orchestra with the names and addresses of all those who attend the concert. Obviously, most of these names are new ones to the orchestra, and they are added to the organization's mailing list for regular concerts in the future.

The Welcome Mat

When new families move into your community, they are faced with the task of finding a new bank, school, dentist, supermarket, auto repair shop, and other resources. Finding out about your theater company might be very low on their list of priorities. You can move that need—and the name of your group—much higher up the list by joining one of the many welcoming organizations that cater to the needs of newcomers. Check with your local chamber of commerce or consult the yellow pages to find out which welcoming programs operate in your area. These are money-making operations, and unless they are new to the community, you will be expected to pay a few dollars to include a brochure or coupon good for discounts on tickets in the welcoming program information packet.

It's Free

Looking for a way to increase audiences at your productions? Consider giving free performances of one-act plays or a musical revue in city parks or at local shopping centers. While your audience is gathered, have company members circulate among them with information about your company. Even better, have tables with sign-up sheets placed strategically around the area so that departing audience members can leave their names and addresses for future mailings.

History 101

Increase ticket sales by educating your audience about the historical or literary context of classic plays or the background of plays that aren't well known. A subscriber or patron newsletter can do this very well, helping to interest potential playgoers who might not otherwise come—or help them explain the play to friends. For example, the *Callboard Companion* of the Omaha Community Playhouse (a sixteen-page publication that goes out to a large mailing list) recently spotlighted a dramatization of Willa Cather's *O Pioneers!* (set in nearby Nebraska) with two articles on the novel and a third on how it was adapted for the Playhouse stage. If you mail similar-looking direct-mail packages regularly, switch paper or ink color. Mailing the same offer to the same list but changing colors boosts response, experts say—people think it's different and they're more likely to open it.

Board Target

Here's an intriguing idea from Liza Zenni, former executive director of San Francisco's Theatre Bay Area. In an issue of the organization's publication, *Callboard,* she writes, "What if we stopped chasing board members for their access to money? What if we scoured our communities for individuals who could deliver audiences instead? Lasso people who are representatives and leaders among the audiences we are seeking, ask them to deliver twenty-five, fifty, or one hundred audience members to each of our productions? How much money would that bring in the door over the course of the season? And what rewards could we reap from community involvement generated by board members whose primary responsibilities are to create a bridge between the community and the theater?"

Using the Churches

Connie Hillesland, a high school speech and drama teacher in Hubbard, Iowa, has found that the best way to make her programs known is to go through local churches. Her speech team and some of her drama students volunteered free performances at church suppers and other events. They discovered that many parishioners stopped going to high school productions once their own children had graduated and they no longer knew any of the people involved in the shows. By sending students into the town to perform, Hillesland reintroduced people to the high school program and its performers. The townspeople now knew some of the student performers, making the high school productions more attractive. The result: Audience numbers have doubled.

Any Way You Can

Some words from the Olympic Theatre Arts newsletter in Sequim, Washington, could easily find their way into your company newsletter as well. Noting how many people in the community never go to the theater, the article suggests a number of reasons: (a) They went once in high school, didn't like it, and haven't returned; (b) They assume community theater is of poor quality; (c) They just don't think about it. We like the suggested solution: If you know people like this, invite them along and pay their way—or go Dutch treat. "Do it any way you can," concludes the article. "Get your friends introduced to an Olympic Theatre Arts performance. You owe it to them and the theater."

Teacher Alert

North Carolina's Asheville Community Theatre offered tickets to *My Fair Lady,* "the perfect companion piece to *Pygmalion,* to area students at a fifty-percent discount for a Thursday evening performance. Area teachers who accompanied their students were admitted free. This works as an excellent audience-development tool, getting young people into the theater, and provides teachers with good discussion material.

Getting to Know Them

Theater companies often wonder where new audiences will come from. Five local arts groups in the Port Angeles, Washington, area went out to find them. They staffed a booth at the local home show under a banner entitled "Local Artists for Local Art." Taking part were the Port Angeles Community Players, Olympic Theatre Arts, Port Angeles Symphony, Port Angeles Children's Theater, and Port Angeles Light Opera Association. According to Geri Zanon in the Olympic Theatre Arts newsletter, the groups put a packet of information together to give to passersby, telling them something about each organization. There were drawings for prizes and an opportunity for people to sign up for any of the organization mailing lists.

"We were busy all day telling people about our organizations and encouraging them to get involved," Zanon says. "Many people were interested in theater and music—some we recognized and some were new to us. We talked to folks of all ages, and many children wanted to know when the next show was and how they could audition."

The booth was a simple and effective way to contact potential audience members, and "equally important, it was an opportunity to talk to each other and share ideas and news," Zanon adds. "After all, whatever we call ourselves, we are all tilling a common soil—the love for theater and the burning desire to share that love with our community."

Families That Play Together

Bringing families to the theater is the idea behind two well-received programs. In March, "Family Week at the Theatre" became the first statewide celebration of theater for New Jersey's young people and their families. During the first week of March, which is also Arts in Education Month, New Jersey's professional theater community offered free tickets to children ages five to eighteen when an adult ticket was purchased. Many theaters hosted backstage tours, workshops, open rehearsals, and other free events designed for multigenerational participation, including twenty-four free performances.

For the Teenagers

Stage One in Louisville, Kentucky, offers Teen Nights, an opportunity for parents and children to attend theater together with activities designed to encourage discussion about plays. For example, a "Backstage Bash" followed a seven o'clock performance of *The Miracle Worker*, with pizza, soft drinks, games, and a guided tour of the Bombard Theater at the Kentucky Center for the Arts. The bash was free with admission to that evening's performance.

One for All

Here's a clever concept that teams performing-arts presenters in Winston-Salem, North Carolina. Area residents may purchase an Arts Card, costing $25, that buys one admission each to The Little Theatre, the Piedmont Opera Theater, and the Winston-Salem Piedmont Triad Symphony. Cards are sold at all three box offices, as well as by the area's arts council.

KEEPING YOUR AUDIENCE

*T*heater companies need repeat customers. As both surveys and common sense tell us, there simply aren't enough potential playgoers out there that we can easily replace a patron who walks in our doors—and then walks out again, never to return. The reservoir is too small to waste any portion of it.

Because almost all companies put on more than one show a season, we need to make sure that theatergoing becomes a habit. We need to make sure that those who have come for the season-opening production of *The Foreigner* also will return for the season-closing production of *Waiting for Godot*.

And the easiest and best way to do that, of course, is with the quality of our productions. If we have done a wonderful job in identifying, finding, and attracting an audience, and then present that audience with a less-than-stellar performance, then we have most definitely shot ourself in the foot. We have taken a "Maybe" and made him or her into a "No." Instead of creating positive word-of-mouth, we will have created negative word-of-mouth, and that is something very hard to overcome. In essence, much of the hard work we have done in developing an audience will have been in vain. So, as one automobile manufacturer puts it, quality must be job one.

But beyond that, we must be responsive to our audiences, willing to adapt to their needs, willing to give them what they are looking for—at the same time that we are producing what we want to produce and can do well. We must make going to the theater a pleasant and engaging experience—before, during, and after the curtain rises and falls. We must understand that while theater may be art, it also is commerce, and so must offer value for the money and give audience members a reason to *want* to come back.

Taking Stock | *24*

While it is important to survey potential audience members and find out who is out there and what they want and what they know about your company, it is equally important to find out about those who do know you and already come to your shows. How are you going to keep them coming if you don't know what they like and don't like about your productions? You need information about them, too, so first you must find out who they are.

Pay Attention to First-Timers

Capturing the names and addresses of your audience is the singlemost important thing you can do in terms of long-term marketing of your company's productions. Whether you use a computerized database or a 3 × 5 card system, you'll find that advertising to these people is the most cost-efficient way of getting the word out about your productions or fundraising projects, or of asking for volunteers. Yet many companies focus almost entirely on season-ticket holders, and do very little in the way of identifying or marketing to single-ticket buyers. If you are not currently working with first-timers, read on.

When the American Conservatory Theatre in San Francisco did its first marketing survey more than ten years ago, it found that most season-ticket subscribers first attended performances on a single-ticket basis. This meant that keeping track of first-timers was vital to the success of the company's season-ticket sales. ACT also found that after these single-ticket purchasers had attended shows for two seasons, they were most likely to convert to season-ticket status.

Only by capturing the names, addresses, and phone numbers of single-ticket purchasers was the company able to mount a special campaign directed toward those people at just the moment when they were most likely to subscribe.

Capturing Names

There are a number of ways to identify first-timers and capture their names, addresses, and phone numbers. The box office/ticket-sales office is the most logical center for this activity.

Arena Stage in Washington, DC, captures the names and addresses of ninety-three percent of its first-time patrons. Within two weeks, Arena volunteers call each person with an offer for a membership that includes a subscription to the theater's magazine, advance notice of special events, and discounts off single tickets to certain productions. About five percent of those called respond positively. Even if a person isn't interested, the theater sends that person direct-mail literature for up to two years, at which time the name is dropped.

With this method, Arena increased its attendance by more than fifty percent over a five-year period. Having a highly visible guestbook in the lobby is another way to capture names and addresses, particularly if you have a volunteer standing by to ask patrons if they would like to be on the list and to answer questions about the company.

You can boost the results even more with a drawing in the lobby. The Tucson Symphony, for example, increased the size of its mailing list by forty percent simply through drawings for prizes at concerts. Many theater companies have had similar success. One overlooked source is group and corporate sales. Most theater companies consider these as only a way to fill the theater, but those who come as part of a group may come back on their own. That's why the Arizona Theatre Company sometimes offers further ticket discounts if the organization purchasing the tickets provides the company with a typewritten list of the names and addresses of all those in the group. Those names go on the mailing list.

Who Are Those People?

25

Once you've found out the names of your audience members, the next step is to find out exactly who they are, how they got there, and what they like and don't like.

Surveying Your Patrons Is a Good Idea Anytime

Taking stock of your company's strengths and weaknesses is a good idea at almost any point. For the all-volunteer Chippewa Valley Theatre Guild of Eau Claire, Wisconsin, the time came at the beginning of its fourteenth year.

"We have a good company," explains Cheryl Starr, a Guild board member at the time of the survey and an associate professor in the Department of Music and Theatre Arts at the University of Wisconsin–Eau Claire. "We do quality work. But the perception was out there that certain needs weren't being met, both of our audience and our volunteers. Some also felt there wasn't enough awareness of the company in the community."

One reason, it was suspected, was that three theater groups use the same performance facility.

"We felt that audiences were not always aware of the difference—they might just be going to the performing-arts center to see a show," Starr explains. "We needed to find out if we were being recognized for our efforts. And we needed to know if our volunteers were happy."

To find out, CVTG asked Starr and John Gribas, an assistant

professor in the Department of Communication and Journalism, to design a survey. It was mailed out to 1,169 season-ticket holders and volunteers in February 1994. Starr explained the survey and its results at a national workshop sponsored by the American Association of Community Theatre in Midland, Texas.

"Our goal was to be exhaustive," Starr explained. "We had lots of questions because we wanted answers from as many different perspectives as possible."

The survey team—which included student researcher Christy Pufall—first considered a telephone survey or lobby interviews. However, these methods might have biased respondents, according to Starr, "because everyone knows one another and they would not have felt completely open in their answers." A related problem is that if company members do the calling, their feelings about certain questions often are obvious even over the phone. (A way to get around this is to hire noncompany members—perhaps students from a local college—to do the calling.)

To be sure respondents felt comfortable answering the questions, they were asked not to write their name on the forms or envelopes. Only one survey was sent to each address regardless of how many people lived there or took part in theater.

What They Asked

The exhaustiveness of the survey is evident from the subjects covered:

1. Personal data of respondent: gender, marital status, community of residence, length of time in community, age, household income, education completed.

2. Have you purchased a CVTG season ticket, and for which season?

3. Respondents were asked to check all productions attended from a list of those presented by local theater organizations the previous year.

4. Respondents were asked to look at a list of previously produced musicals and check those they would like to see again.

5. Respondents were asked to review a list of plays being considered for production and check those they would like to see. Space also was provided for the respondents' own suggestions.

6. Have you donated to the company, and if you have ceased to do so, why?

7. Respondents who have volunteered with the company were asked in what areas they had done so.

8. How did you first hear of CVTG (friend, someone at work, newspaper, etc.)?

9. How do you receive information about production dates and times (friend, someone at work, newspaper, etc.)?

10. In the main body of the survey, the respondent was presented with a list of thirty-five statements to rank on a scale of one (strongly disagree) to five (strongly agree). Examples: "CVTG should do more serious plays," "The lasagna dinner is a great way to thank volunteers," "CVTG season tickets are reasonably priced," "CVTG needs a separate phone for ticket reservations," "CVTG should have a larger paid staff," "The same people are always in leadership roles in CVTG productions," and "Parking is a major problem for CVTG patrons."

11. Respondents were asked open-ended questions such as, "When I think of the Chippewa Valley Theatre Guild, the first things that come to my mind are. . . ."

12. The survey ended with open-ended evaluations of volunteer experiences. Specifically, the respondent was asked to "reflect on a specific time when your volunteer experience with CVTG was particularly rewarding/satisfying or particularly frustrating/dissatisfying."

How They Did It

The eight-page survey was long, Starr admits, but "we tested it and found that It took only eight minutes to fill out. Besides, this was possibly the only time we would get a chance to conduct a survey like this for some time."

Despite its length, the survey had a fifty-four-percent response rate—627 out of 1,169.

"We got the word out through the company newsletter that a survey was on its way. Since its length was a concern, we explained the time to complete it so it wouldn't be a surprise, and the deadline for returning. The next newsletter had a note reminding people to return the form."

In addition, each questionnaire was accompanied by an introductory letter from the CVTG survey team.

"We sent out the surveys on Friday by bulk mail," Starr says. "On Monday, we had the first sixteen back. A return of ten to fifteen percent is considered good, and we had that by Tuesday. (Some professionals in the field consider that rate only marginal.) The return rate was forty-nine percent by the deadline date. After the reminder in the newsletter, it rose to fifty-four percent."

What They Found

The survey gave CVTG a great deal of useful information. For example, "We were able to construct a 'typical volunteer' profile," Starr explains—"female, married, thirty-six to forty-five years old, an Eau Claire resident, twenty-plus years in the community, $35,000 to $50,000 household income, four-year college degree."

While such a profile wasn't entirely a surprise, there were some unexpected results. For example, donation level did not correlate with income level; that is, the wealthiest were not necessarily the most generous.

Sometimes what wasn't said was as instructive as what was. A greater percentage of subscribers responded than volunteers. Considering that one purpose was to gauge volunteer interest, this relatively low participation may indicate an area of concern.

CVTG put much of the information to use immediately. Responses about play choice, for example, went to the play-reading committee. The respondents' first choice, *Arsenic and Old Lace*, was scheduled for the 1995–96 season. (However, Starr points out that because only titles were given as choices, respondents unfamiliar with them might have given a negative response or none at all. In the future, she says, the group may hand out a questionnaire in the lobby with titles and a brief synopsis of each.)

Results also were used in developing a new brochure, volunteer job descriptions, and the season package of plays. Marketing efforts focused on the responses to "How did you first hear of us?" and looked at ways to improve community awareness of the group.

"We also found a large geographical spread of our audience, which indicates a potential in marketing to areas outside Eau Claire itself," Starr says.

Was the time and effort expended worth it? Definitely, Starr says. "We've been a part of the Chippewa Valley's arts scene for fifteen years. Like other groups our age, we have reached a point where the initial momentum has slowed, and business as usual is no longer a choice. Most of us felt that we needed more information to help us plot our direction. The survey results have helped us do exactly that."

Words to the Wise

If your company is considering a survey, Starr has some advice. She suggests posing both open- and closed-ended questions. Closed-ended questions (for example, checking "yes" or "no" or grading on a scale of one to five) give the most control over the survey and the most consistent results—but they also presume you already know the possible responses. Open-ended questions (those allowing the respondents to choose their own words) allow more freedom and often uncover hidden problems or concerns. However, because each person responds differently, they are much more difficult to compare.

"Use shorter questions whenever possible," Starr advises. "And avoid negatives in the question. If you do use negatives, underline or capitalize the negative word so that it's clear what you mean."

Questionnaires should be visually uncluttered, she suggests. Make instructions on marking choices clear, whether it be fill-in, underline, circle, or check mark. The CVTG survey team showed the survey to friends (not on the company mailing list) to see if there were any problems of clarity.

Starr points out that the survey asked the same question in several different ways. For example, respondents were asked to rank their feelings on these statements: "The same people are always in leadership roles in CVTG productions," "The same people are always cast in CVTG productions," "It is difficult to feel like you're part of 'the group' at CVTG," and "CVTG is a closed organization." Note that each statement speaks to the same issue. Comparing responses indicates the depth of feeling.

Lewis Copulsky, Managing Partner of the Lewis & Clark Research firm, cautions against using what could be biased wording in the statements. It might be better to ask, he says, "how easy or difficult is it to feel like you're part of the group at CVTG."

As a cost-saving measure, the company provided respondents with addressed but not stamped envelopes. Survey professionals normally suggest putting a stamp on the return envelope to increase participation. Return-reply envelopes ("No Postage Necessary") are another suggestion, and you don't have to pay the postage for those not used. (However, you do need a special permit from the post office.)

CVTG also chose to distribute surveys by third-class mail. While its response rate was impressively high, professionals argue that first-class mail is best, addressed directly on the envelope (not a label).

Starr points to several areas she believes could have been

improved. For example, the survey asked in what capacities respondents volunteered, but did not ask them to rank them in importance.

"We might have twenty-five people who checked 'set-building' but we don't know if this was their main focus. They might have been actors in the production who also helped build. So the final numbers didn't really give us as good a picture of our volunteers as we had hoped."

The final page, asking open-ended questions about volunteer experiences, didn't elicit many responses, Starr says, and might have been better as a separate survey.

It's important to remember that a mail survey self-selects the respondents—people who like to fill out questionnaires, those with the time to do so, those with a strong interest in the company or in theater, or those with an axe to grind. While the results are useful, they may not be as broadly representative as a random telephone survey. Research has shown, though, that especially when you approach response rates of fifty percent and above, views of nonrespondents are not substantially different from those of respondents. As a general overview of volunteer and patron attitudes, CVTG's survey is a useful tool.

Want to Improve? Ask the Experts | 26

*I*f you're wondering what you're doing well and where you need to improve, go to the experts—your patrons. That's what the Little Theatre of Wilkes-Barre, Pennsylvania, did recently. A survey was mailed to patrons asking them to "Tell us how to make Little Theatre better than ever!" Surveys could be returned by mail or turned in at the theater.

While this method won't produce statistically valid results, it does provide valuable input. People can write out their thoughts instead of simply answering yes or no, or grading only on a sliding scale. You're apt to find out things you wouldn't learn otherwise.

Survey questions include:

■ Concerning the exterior appearance of the theater, what would you add, delete, change for the better?

■ Concerning the interior appearance of the theater, what would you add, delete, change for the better?

■ Regarding the quality of customer service as a patron, how do you rate our staff (scale of one to ten). How could it be improved?

■ What kind of productions would you like to see more of (be specific)?

■ Do you feel that you are getting your money's worth from experiencing a show at Little Theatre? (This might be expanded to include "Why?")

■ How would you rate the quality of our productions? Performance (one to ten), Technical Quality (one to ten).

■ What do you like most about coming to the theater?

■ What do you dislike most about coming to the theater?

■ How do you feel Little Theatre can better support the community?

■ Are you or have you ever been interested in onstage, backstage, or front-office involvement? Which area?

Also requested was the patron's sex, length of time as a Little Theatre patron, and hometown. Among other things, this information would be useful in evaluating some of the other responses.

We suspect the twin questions of what the patron likes most and dislikes most about coming to the theater would provide the most interesting (and useful) information. Here's where you can find those good points you can promote in your marketing and publicity material, and the bad points you can work to overcome.

Consider Yourself at Home | 27

No matter who your audience members are, they like to be treated well. They want to be comfortable in your theater and they want to be appreciated. They are our guests, after all. We must remember that we need to treat them that way.

Eighteen Ways to Make Your Audience Want to Come Back Again and Again

SARAH STARR

Your advertising was a success: your theater is packed. But will your patrons return? To keep them coming back, you must give them a high-quality performance, of course, but also an enjoyable experience as well. Follow this checklist to help make your audience feel comfortable and at home, and you will find yourself with consistently full houses.

Well in Advance

1. *Check your sight lines.* Do not sell seats with an inadequate view of the stage. Even if you reduce the price of "pillar seats," the resulting stiff necks will make for disappointed patrons.

2. *Clearly mark theater entrances.* Make sure they are well lighted.

3. *Don't overbook.* If you cannot manage multiple-ticket outlets without errors, restrict your ticket sales to a single office. (Some theater companies set aside house seats for the director and other staff, selling these when necessary.)

4. *Print extra information in your programs.* Present confusing characters—for example, explain the various relationships in Shakespeare's *The Comedy of Errors.* When possible, include photographs. Clarify scene changes. Introduce the actors, author, or play. This not only keeps early arrivals occupied, but lets patrons identify more with your production.

5. *Stroll through your lobby and restrooms.* Are the walls clean? Does the theater smell musty? Is your curtain spotted? Would the patrons' seats make them wince before sitting down? Pull out the cleaning supplies and go to work; your theater should look, smell, and feel clean.

Before the Curtain Rises

6. *Vacuum or sweep.* Clean the parking lot and sidewalk as well.

7. *Make it easy for audience members to find their seats.* Are seat numbers clearly marked? Review seat numbers with your ushers. They should be able to offer clear directions.

8. *Check for intrusive sounds.* Some years ago, the St. Louis Opera Company performed unexpectedly to the accompaniment of a dance band upstairs. Make sure you won't be doing the same.

During the Play

9. *Control interruptions.* If patrons enter late, usher them to seats in the back even if they have assigned seats. Politely reprimand constant whisperers who are obviously bothering their neighbors. (And, of course, don't allow backstage noise.)

10. *Enforce all policies,* especially "no smoking." The few people you may offend will be far outweighed by the people who breathe a sigh of relief.

11. *Announce any long curtain delays.*

12. *If possible, keep your theater at seventy degrees year-round.* Make the theater a welcome escape from the weather outside.

Intermission

13. *Don't rush your audience.* Give them plenty of advance warning of curtains: flick the lights, ring chimes, or announce the time a few minutes before the curtain will rise.

14. *If possible, open back and outside doors during intermissions for ventilation.*

15. *Provide free refreshments.* Tea and crumpets, punch and cookies, or just styrofoam cups by the water fountain—give whatever your budget allows. People are delighted to receive something for free. Simple courtesies make a difference. Remember that you are not just out to make money on this specific performance, but also to get audiences to return.

When It's Over

16. *Sustain the mood.* If appropriate, play music as the audience files out.

17. *Search the auditorium for lost items* after each performance. Return any identifiable articles.

18. *Acknowledge all complaints.* If the complaint is valid, write to the aggrieved patron and explain what corrective actions you plan to take. If nothing else, thank your customer for drawing your attention to the problem. If patrons feel you have listened and taken their advice, they are more likely to become firm supporters.

It's important to entertain an audience, but a television can do that. Don't just give your patrons something to watch—show them hospitality. Give them even more than the comforts of home.

28 The Benefits Package

It's axiomatic that we treat our guests differently than we treat strangers. And over the recent past, theaters have learned to treat our steady customers—our season-ticket holders—better, perhaps, than we treat the single-ticket buyer. We want to offer them privileges and give them perks that the casual patron doesn't receive—so that they can perceive the benefits of regular attendance. Over the next few chapters, you'll find several ways to do that.

Ticket Vouchers Please Both the Theater and Businesses

"*L*ike a good utility infielder, it covers a lot of bases."

That's the way Keith Martin of North Carolina's Charlotte Repertory Theatre describes Flextik. The idea is simple: Businesses can purchase tickets (more accurately, vouchers for tickets) for unspecified performances, providing them with a welcome spur-of-the-moment gift for clients, customers, colleagues, or employees.

Sold in blocks of ten tickets for $200, Flextiks can be given singly, in groups, or in the full block. Each Flextik then can be exchanged by the recipient for one ticket to any Charlotte Rep performance, subject to availability.

Named for the flexibility of their use, Flextiks accommodate the often haphazard schedules of employees and clients.

"You might not know until the last minute that a client will stay over or a guest needs an evening's entertainment or it's someone's birthday," said Martin. "Flextik works extremely well. The corporation can pull tickets from the block and guests can make reservations to fit their schedule. We've been able to accommodate a 7 P.M. request for that night's 8 P.M. curtain."

Reservations are still a good idea, especially for a show

that may be sold out. To reduce the chance of empty seats from Flextik leftovers, all seats are released to walk-up buyers at 5 P.M. the evening of each show.

"We get calls from people who tell us they have only three Flextiks left and don't want to be caught short, so they order another block of ten. These are all good seats; we pull twice the number of house seats we need for emergencies and make half of them available for Flextik."

Purchasing businesses see Flextik as a bargain. For $20 per voucher, the buyer is promised some of the best seats in the house at a price that represents a savings of five to eighteen percent over a single ticket bought at the box office.

The company hopes, as well, that once introduced to the high quality of its productions, audience members would likely return on their own. Few out-of-town clients, entertained by *Forever Plaid* in September, would not seek tickets to *Laughter on the 23rd Floor* on a return visit to the city the following June, goes the logic.

Flextiks can be the first step to a partnership with a local business. In addition, the vouchers provide revenue to the theater company well in advance of an actual production.

Marketed as "Business Entertainment That Makes Good Sense" in an attractive promotional brochure, Flextik is a concept that makes sense for many theater companies. It's a program in which everybody wins: the theater, the buyer, and the recipient.

29 | Behind the Scenes

Backstage Tours Can Do Your Company a World of Good—If You Know How to Do Them

NANCIANNE PFISTER

"*T*he Bonstelle [theater] is supposedly haunted by the ghost of Jessie Bonstelle, so all our tours include a couple of ghost stories," says Wendy Evans of Wayne State University in Detroit.

Even without a resident wraith to show off, your company may be thinking of opening your backstage area to the general public, local students, season-ticket holders, or donors. We wanted to know the reasons for bringing visitors to that part of your facility. And who gets the tour? How does it work? Is it safe? What are the benefits? Hazards?

We posed those questions and more to five theater organizations: a regional children's theater, a group of renovated vaudeville houses, the oldest U.S. Shakespearean festival, the biggest community theater in the country, and a large university. (If your company is smaller and your production area less technically sophisticated, your group still can offer tours. Audiences are interested in learning how shows are produced and will be fascinated by things you've taken for granted for years.)

We also checked with a firm that deals in theatrical insurance. What if a guest trips on a cable? What if someone leans on the rigging or breaks a chair loaned for the current production?

The responses were informative.

Why Do It?

The reasons for offering tours are diverse. Some companies just want to make their audiences feel more at home.

"Our backstage tour is a big part of [our operation]," says Deborah Elliott of the Oregon Shakespeare Festival. "It is one of the best opportunities for theatergoers to get an overall feeling for what we do. They are allowed into places usually used only by actors, designers, and technicians. It makes our patrons feel special."

Ginny Winsor of Omaha Community Playhouse agrees: "We offer backstage tours because people always like to feel they are in the know and catch a glimpse of how we do this magic of theater. Getting to see back stage gives them that feeling."

A very different purpose is served by tours Wayne State University provides for a group that raises money for the theater, called The Understudies. The tours give the group a firmer understanding of the theater so they can answer questions prospective donors may have. Seattle Children's Theatre offers tours to its board members for a similar reason.

On the other hand, Cleveland's Playhouse Square sees its tours for the general public as a promotional tool. As Director of Theater Operations John Hemsath tells us, "We are a not-for-profit group. Half of our funding comes directly from the public. This is a chance for them to come to the theater without a ticket." The hope is that, feeling included, they will return to purchase tickets for a future production.

Clearly, *why* tours are offered is closely linked to the question of *who* takes the backstage tour. Like most other colleges, Wayne State provides tours of its facility to prospective students. It also includes tours with its student matinee program, as does Seattle Children's Theatre.

"We have a local college that offers a degree in theater administration. It's important for those students to know all the aspects of production," says SCT's Susan O'Connell. "We also give tours to high school theater classes. We may have ten different tours a week, depending on who is taking the tour."

Omaha Community Playhouse also offers different tours, according to Ginny Winsor, including many for school groups, "but we also try to attract service clubs—Rotary, Kiwanis, etc.—with lunch and tours so they will begin to feel a vested interest in OCP. These clubs and the businesses they represent become strong supporters of our programming."

What to Show

On the question of what to show backstage guests, there seems to be general agreement that more is better. In Cleveland, John Hemsath says, "Whatever we can show, we do. We begin with a slide show that gives the history of all four theaters—originally vaudeville houses—in Playhouse Square. It goes on to show the years of vacancy and then the restoration process that has been completed in three of the four buildings. The tour takes about two hours."

"For a tour to be educational, it should show how all the elements of a production work together," Seattle's O'Connell says. "Our tours are limited because our scene shop and costume shop are off-site. Our new on-site tech pavilion will have floor-to-ceiling windows so people can see the more intricate aspects of production."

The tour at WSU changes according to the interests of the touring group. If it's another university class, the focus will be related to the course content. After showing the backstage facilities, visitors may be treated to lighting demonstrations or some other area of technical interest.

In Oregon, the hour-and-forty-five-minute tour begins at The Black Swan, the 140-seat black-box theater. Tour guides talk about the facility and about the kinds of plays performed in this intimate space. The tour then moves to the outdoor Elizabethan Theatre, which boasts extraordinary acoustics that are demonstrated for visitors as they stand on stage. If their tour guide is an actor, guests may hear some personal stories of what it's like to perform in the rain or to compete with bats, bugs, and the Big Dipper for the attention of the audience. Before moving to the six-hundred-seat state-of-the-art Angus Bowmer Theatre, the group sees the green room, dressing rooms, wig room, and costume/wardrobe areas.

This tour is a ticketed event of the festival, with admission prices ranging from $6.30 to $9.50. At SCT, the charge is $25 for a group. If the tour is being conducted as a reward or incentive to donors, the charge is waived. Playhouse Square tours are free to the public on the first Saturday and Sunday of each month except in January and August. For $50, groups of ten or more can arrange for a private tour on another day. Omaha Community Playhouse doesn't charge for its backstage tours because, says Ginny Winsor, "The more bodies we can get into any part of the theater, the better. If we can give them a sense of ownership, they'll come back to us as volunteers and ticket-buyers."

At the Oregon Shakespeare Festival, which hosts up to 130 tour-goers each day, tours average twenty-five to thirty people, the same number assigned at Seattle Children's Theatre. SCT's O'Connell notes that business seems to come in spurts, with a big crowd in March and then almost no one until May.

Tour Guides

If you've ever been trapped with an ineffectual docent or tour guide, you can appreciate the need to train backstage guides. The level of instruction varies from "semiformalized" at WSU to "intensive train-ing" at the Oregon Shakespeare Festival. Omaha's volunteers are trained, with a script. No one we talked with allows their guides to wing it.

"Our guides are given basic information, then allowed to person-alize it according to their experience and the tour group," says Wayne State's Wendy Evans, adding, "Whether the tour is led by a student, a technician, or a faculty member, we always try to have students around to talk with guests, especially if the guests are prospective students."

At Playhouse Square, training began as a six-hour lecture. As time went by, one volunteer rose to the top and developed a manual with transcripts and an outline. He is now in charge of training and assigning the volunteer guides.

Many Oregon Shakespeare Festival tours are conducted by ac-tors. Stage managers, costume builders, house managers, and other audience-service staff also guide visitors. Because guests are en-couraged to ask questions, guides must be prepared with a variety of information.

"Our tour guides have intensive training," says the Festival's Deborah Elliott. "They have to know the history of the theaters and of the festival. They must know the schedule of the current season, in-cluding the directors, designers, and number of performances. They are asked about casting and about our annual budget. They are often asked how many people are involved or what the economic impact on the city is."

Liability

Good hosts are responsible for the safety of their guests. What are the risks of allowing visitors back stage in your theater? Will your liability insurance costs rise when you open your work areas? How do you protect your visitors and your company?

William J. Haycook is an agent for liability insurance designed for theater companies by the Ponta, Castle and Ingram Agency. In general, he says, "your cost goes up as your risk goes up, but there is no single answer. Backstage tours are covered in our AACT [American Association of Community Theatre] insurance program, as such tours are seen as a 'not unforeseen risk.' They may be covered by other insurance policies as well, but it is always best to check with your current agent to verify coverage."

While insurance is a good thing, it's a better thing to prevent accidents that would result in a claim. Haycook offers some commonsense advice if you're considering offering a tour.

"As with any liability exposure," he says, "there are things you can do to minimize the risk of injury: use only experienced tour guides, keep all areas well lighted, use glo-tape to show the actual tour route, review tour ground rules with participants, and clearly mark areas that are off-limits to visitors."

SCT's O'Connell agrees: "We have a very controlled tour. Perhaps because we're a children's theater, we're more aware of the danger zones. We have what we call our 'kid patrol' to keep people from wandering into places they should not be. We make sure every place is safe to walk through."

There is little question that backstage tours are good public relations, whether to reward volunteers, show need to potential donors, or just give your patrons a sense of inclusion. Whether your company offers such a tour depends on what benefits you might derive from it.

But one thing seems certain: A tour's success lies in the hands of the tour guides. They must be informed, enthusiastic, and prepared for anything. Even a ghost.

Extending the Season-Ticket Season

30

*I*f you think that season-ticket sales end before the first production, take a look at this clever marketing idea from California's Woodland Opera House, which puts on a variety of plays in its season. Theatergoers who attended its first production received a flyer inserted into the printed program. *"Save Your Stub!"* proclaims the flyer headline. "If you enjoyed this performance, you can still obtain season tickets and reap the benefits of our season-ticket holders." A season-ticket order form fills the bottom half of the $8^1/_2 \times 11$ sheet. The flyer then lists seven benefits:

1. The best seats in the house. Your seats are reserved before individual tickets go on sale to the general public. And you can renew those seats year after year.

2. Convenience—your tickets are mailed right to you. This means no trips to the box office, no sold-out performances, no worries.

3. When you subscribe, you become a supporter of one of the most exciting theater companies in northern California. You will receive inside information through our bimonthly newsletter and invitations to special events. And you will

receive the right to vote for the Opera House's own version of the Tonys, Oscars, and Emmys—the Chesley Awards.

4. A savings over single-ticket prices. Your entertainment dollar can go farther. Order a couple of extra season tickets for friends.

5. Discount and first choice of seating for Variety [i.e., guest] Artists performances.

6. Ticket-exchange privileges up to twenty-four hours in advance of your scheduled performance. You won't have to miss a single show.

7. Free replacement of lost or misplaced tickets. Simply contact the box office in advance of your regularly scheduled performance.

If you like this approach, we suggest two improvements. First, the third item should lead with its strongest selling point, the newsletter and invitations. Second, the reason for saving ticket stubs needs to be made clear up front. It's not mentioned until the instructions for filling out the order form (and it's not on the order form itself).

A Newsletter Can Increase Audiences

31

A newsletter for your customers is a valuable market-ing tool. It can help you sell more tickets, build audi-ence loyalty, and give your company more credibility. Here are seven suggestions to help you.

1. *Put yourself in the reader's place.* What kind of information are they likely to need? What subjects will interest them? However, don't be shy about putting in information that you think the reader should know.

2. *Short stories are easier to read.* They also make the design more attractive because you can break up the text with white space.

3. *Write in personal terms* so that customers will feel you're talking to them. Use "you," "your," and "you're" whenever possible. (You'll note that's the way we phrase most of our articles in *Stage Directions.*) If you can work in the names of patrons, so much the better.

4. *Include something that invites customers to respond,* such as special promotions, ways to request additional information, or a ballot to indicate interest in possible future productions.

5. *Give patrons a name to call*, rather than an impersonal phone number.

6. *Keep your sales pitch low-key and offer lots of useful information.* Avoid hyperbole ("a wonderful, exciting show"). Instead, tell your readers why the show is wonderful or exciting. Help them understand how to best contact you with questions, give them parking tips, or ideas on nearby restaurants (including cost and menu). Suggest alternate routes if traffic is often busy.

7. *Make readers feel like insiders.* Give them background on regularly featured players, how you choose shows, or plans for future seasons. Use photos of regularly featured players when writing about them if you can reproduce photos well in your newsletter. It's more personal and people will immediately be able to key in to the subject.

Include background of the upcoming show—original opening date and place, original cast members of note, interesting trivia about the history of its productions, or evolution of the script/score itself. Not only will it spark interest where there might not have been any before, but your patrons will appreciate "looking good" as they share the information with their friends!

Marketing to the Converted | 32

Nancy Rothman

*H*ere are three ways to market your theater company to those who already know it—your ticket-buyers. Of course, these are only the tip of the iceberg; there are numerous effective and inexpensive ways to build and retain your audience.

1. *Inform your faithful patrons*—your best audience. Find a way to record the names, addresses, and phone numbers not only of subscribers, but also of single-ticket buyers (perhaps keeping a list as they call to reserve tickets). Try a raffle at performances with goods provided by local merchants to capture walk-in names.

Previous audience members form your primary list. Send a flyer and follow up with a phone call to this list before your season begins. Your regular subscribers generally will be delighted to hear from you and appreciate the reminder to renew their subscription.

2. *Start or strengthen a "Friends of the Theater" group*. Many faithful audience members identify with your theater company as "their" company. They will often reminisce about

the number of years they have attended and the major performances of their favorite actors.

Add a special reception or an after-the-show cabaret to a performance for "friends" who have bought full subscriptions, purchased advertising, or who have donated in some way to the theater. Many would be thrilled to meet the actors they have admired and feel that much more a part of your theater family. (Some groups give free tickets to advertisers who purchase a quarter-page ad or more, or who donate more than a specific amount.)

3. *Develop a brief marketing survey to be handed out to your audience.* What do patrons like about your season? What don't they like? What would they like to see more of? How did they hear about the group or the production? This additional information can help you plan your next season. There also may be small things that are troubling to your patrons that you can easily rectify, like the refreshments you serve (or don't serve) or the sight-line problems of particular seats.

How to Design a | 33
Great Season
Brochure

Perhaps the single most important device we employ for keeping our audiences coming back each year is the season brochure. This tells our audiences why they should continue coming and what they will miss if they don't come. This mentions all the special perks of economy and convenience they will receive if they come to the theater regularly. This is, in other words, our single biggest enticement.

We send a copy of the season brochure to all those who have bought season tickets before or have expressed interest in buying season tickets. We send it to those who have bought single tickets in the past in the hope that we can turn them into multiple purchasers or season-ticket holders.

The season brochure carries a lot of weight and a lot of our hopes and expectations. It must, therefore, measure up to the highest standards. Here's how to do it right.

Know Your Reader, Plan Every Inch, Keep It Simple

*I*f your theater company is like most, the season brochure is your single most important marketing tool. Because so much rides on this brochure, it's important to understand exactly what works—and why.

General Principles

Let's start with two seemingly contradictory observations. First, brochures often carry a lasting message. At least one study shows that half the people who receive a brochure will save it or pass it on to someone else. The more attractive and informative, the more likely the piece is to be saved. So it makes sense to plan and execute your season brochure with as much care as possible.

However, while the message may be lasting, the reader's attention is not. Again, studies indicate that when people pick up a brochure, most skim it, skipping around rather than reading from front to back. That makes putting together brochures a challenge, because you can't assume that the reader will read the information in the order it's placed on the page. Instead, each section of the brochure has to stand on its own to grab the reader's attention and provide necessary information.

There's no one right way to design a brochure. However, designers, printers, and direct-mail experts give us three basic rules: Make it attractive, easy to read, and simple to follow. Here are some suggestions gleaned from these same sources.

Text: Short and Sweet

There's no great secret to the writing that you find in good brochures: The text is short and to the point. Readers don't want to work hard to find what they need to know. So put yourself in the reader's place. What specific words are most likely to interest them? What kind of information are they likely to need? And what will they want to know first?

Write in personal terms so that readers will feel you're talking to them. Use "you," "your," and "you're" whenever possible, as in "You'll experience a whole world of entertainment."

Avoid empty hyperbole when describing each show in the season. Don't say the show is wonderful and exciting. Tell *why* the show is wonderful or exciting ("You'll gasp as the detective uncovers the murderer in the spine-tingling climax").

Be honest. Don't oversell your capabilities or set up false expectations.

Finally, when you write, keep in mind that short sections are easier to read. They also make the brochure design more inviting because you can break up the text with white space.

Envelope or Self-Mailer?

Most companies produce brochures that are mailed without envelopes. Such a "self-mailer" saves the cost of an envelope and may cut postage costs by reducing weight.

However, there is something to be said for the more personal look of an envelope addressed to the patron. So if you use an envelope, be sure to make it part of the sales package. If the envelope lacks interest, the brochure has to work that much harder. One simple solution is to buy envelopes with a distinctive color that also works with the brochure.

Whether you use an envelope or a self-mailer, the outside should feature an illustration, theme, or line of copy from the brochure as a "teaser" (a few words that compel the reader to open the piece). A teaser might read something like "America's favorite musical" or "You'll die laughing," followed by the words, "See inside for more details" in smaller print.

As many direct-marketers point out, the most important thing is to get the reader to open your brochure and have a look. Design the outside of your mailer with that in mind. (And if you go to the expense of using an envelope, don't defeat the purpose by using a mailing label; type or print directly on the envelope. Studies show that mail that looks individually addressed gets a better response.)

Attention-Grabbing

The brochure's cover must grab the reader's attention. Use a strong photo or graphic that illustrates a single idea or concept. (See page 120 for more about photos). Keep words to a minimum and make the type big and easy to read. Like the design itself, the words should be simple, intriguing, and inviting.

Imagine you are passing out your brochure in some busy spot and it must attract attention as people stroll by. If your cover wouldn't grab *their* attention, it probably won't capture your intended audience's interest either.

Format and Size

You may gain visibility if your brochure is different in shape and size from others that arrive in the mail. Study what your competitors are doing. Use a different format—one that helps you organize the information for your readers—or use a different way of folding.

One different approach is the calendar-brochure. This makes for a more complex brochure, but its size and shape do call attention to it. A calendar from the Woodland Opera House is larger ($8^1/_2 \times 5^1/_2$ inches, folded) and easier to read, while a more colorful brochure from the Topeka Civic Theater fits pocket or purse ($4^1/_4 \times 7^1/_4$ inches, folded).

One warning: The postal service will not accept just any size piece—nor will every standard envelope. Dimensions also affect the price; odd sizes can mean waste when the printer trims to size. Before spending money on a nonstandard-size brochure, check with both your printer and the post office.

Design Considerations

Design is more than the way text and graphics are laid out on the page. Design also projects an image of your company and its season. You want to sell entertainment, fun, excitement, intellectual stimulation, and quality. A colorful bronchure from the Market House Theatre in Paducah, Kentucky, does all these things well.

Be sure to consider the graphic sophistication of your reader. Arts patrons tend to be well educated and are accustomed to high-quality printing. If they're not familiar with your company, they may make a value judgment based on the quality (i.e., writing, paper, photography, and color) of your printed brochure.

Color

Sure, it's expensive, but people are used to seeing color. And studies again indicate that color does add to the effectiveness of a printed document.

Two colors are fine, and you can use tints (*screens* in printer language) to vary the richness of the colors. For example, a 50-percent screen of red gives you pink. You also can overlap screens of two colors to give the impression of three colors: Red and green overlapped become brown, yellow and blue become green, and so on.

One of the most effective uses of color we've seen is the Market House Theatre's season brochure. It uses three colors on one side and four-color process on the other. Four-color processing is more expensive, but this piece uses no photographs and so avoids additional prepress work that can add substantially to the cost.

Using Photos

Photographs give information quickly and memorably. Usually, a posed shot is better than one actually shot in performance, where focus and lighting can be troublesome. Come in close on the actors (preferably no more than three); keep distracting backgrounds to a minimum.

Avoid grouping several photographs into a collage; one strong photo is more likely to grab the reader. If you use more than one photo, make the strongest photo much larger than the others.

Put a caption on every photograph or other illustration; research shows that people look at a photo first, then the caption. Captions should sell, not merely describe.

When choosing photos, one designer suggests thinking how each photograph would work if your brochure were printed in a foreign language. In other words, ignore the words themselves and look at what the photo "says" about your company and its productions.

Other Art

Consider simple graphics or eye-catching illustrations to depict themes of plays. In fact, illustrations often work better than photos. They can be less literal than a photo and thus indicate a broader range of qualities.

Testimonials

If you're still in the process of building community recognition, use testimonials—comments from critics or audience members. Remember to clear it with the person being quoted before you print a testimonial. (If you aren't currently collecting testimonials, put in a "Comment Box" in the lobby with a supply of three-by-five cards.)

Order Form

If the cover is the entry point to the brochure, the order form is the exit point. If the reader gets this far, they are likely prospects. But it's here that many brochures are weakest.

The most common complaint about order forms is that they are too complicated. If you want good results, the form *must* be easy to understand. Keep details to the essentials. The design should lead the ticket-buyer through each step of the process so that you collect all essential information.

Another complaint is that order forms are too small, making it hard to write legibly. We like the format of the Market House Theatre, which presents its subscription information in a vertical, easy-to-read format. The part filled out by the subscriber, on the other hand, is horizontal, giving plenty of room to write clearly.

The best way to tell if your order form does its job well is to test it. Give copies to people who are unfamiliar with it and have them try to fill it out in your presence. Observe what they look for and how easily they find it. Be on the alert for signs of confusion. And listen to what they say.

Talk to your box-office or ticket-order people. Find out what mistakes purchasers make most often. Then review your order form to see if it can be improved to reduce such problems. Run all forms past the box-office manager to make sure the form is practical and contains all necessary information.

Review Results

When the subscription period ends, review the brochure and its impact. Keep what works, discard or improve what doesn't. Keep a file of brochures from other sources (theater-related or not) that have caught your attention, so that you'll always have new ideas from which to draw.

Finally, think of your brochure as a theatrical production. Invest in it all the care and imagination that you would invest in a play. Readers can and do make a connection between the quality of your printed piece and the quality of your productions.

Build a Better Brochure | 34

Learn from Those Who've Done It Well— With Different Techniques and Budgets

Designing a great season brochure is always a challenge. There's a lot to say—play names, dates, schedules, ticket information, and much more—and not much space to say it. In a competitive environment, with many other publicity handouts begging for the customer's attention, the effective brochure must convey its information clearly, interestingly, and within your budgetary means.

Here are some tips we've gathered from looking at many different season brochures from across the country.

An unusual size or shape gains attention. Cincinnati's Fahrenheit Theatre Company has a square-shaped mailer with a great cover tease ("Seduction, Mischief, Murder, Magic, and Mayhem . . . ") and a delightfully devilish Shakespeare. To cut costs, the piece is designed with two colors on one side and black only on the other.

Centre Stage from Greenville, South Carolina, uses a repetitive design element that is highly effective, leading the reader through the season, play by play. With very little text, the names of the plays are highlighted. The design element—a pointing finger—also makes production photos unnecessary.

A mailer can be highly effective using just two colors. (When you're using two colors, remember you can use almost any two.) The small size ($4^3/_4 \times 8^1/_4$ inches, folded) of the Charlotte Repertory mailer is pleasing and practical for display, but the ticket order form is a bit cramped.

A clever two-color brochure from the Kearney Community Theatre in Nebraska unfolds to reveal a string of tickets, one for each show. This gives each production individual attention while still linking the season together. A lighter-color paper would make the smaller type easier to read.

A four-color theme piece (the cover asks "Are you game?")—a mailer from the Sacramento Theatre Company—is clever, yet its complexity never overpowers the main purpose of highlighting each show in the season. The order blank covers the full width of the piece, making it easy to fill out (although a bit more difficult for the patron to cut and fold).

One color needn't be boring. A nicely designed mailer from the Pennsylvania Playhouse is simple and attractive (as well as inexpensive to produce), with the separate information placed in easy-to-find blocks. Individualized artwork calls attention to each show title.

A stunning piece from Nebraska's Lincoln Community Playhouse uses black ink for the text and an eye-catching metallic copper ink for accent. Each panel (roughly $4^1/_4$ inches wide) features two plays in narrow columns, yet never looks cramped. The illustrations for each play are simple and don't compete with the titles, but rather complement them.

The KISS concept ("Keep It Simple, Stupid") covers a wide range of territory, but none more so than with season brochures. Sometimes we get so involved with designing that we forget that what readers *really* want is information.

While it's true that your season brochure should be well designed and capture attention, the bottom line is simple: It should be easy to read and follow, do a good job of selling your season, and allow patrons to find the information they need—and respond.

Brochures can be highly sophisticated or more basic two-color pieces with uncomplicated graphics. However, all of them should have uncluttered designs that are attractive, readable, and powerful.

When 35
Nothing Works

What if nothing works? What if, despite all your best efforts, wonderful productions, welcoming atmosphere, scintillating brochures, and splendid subscriber perks, some past patrons simply do not come to your theater any more? What do you do then?

It's Called Retention

R etention is a buzzword in academic circles, referring to a school's ability to hang on to students after they enroll, and specifically to efforts to reduce the dropout rate. Theater companies have dropouts too. One company took stock recently and found the following about its mailing list of 3,384 names:

Attended in 1996 but not since	219
Attended in 1997 but not since	303
Attended in 1998	988
	___
Total since 1996	1,510
Total inactive	1,874

The company began keeping track of patron ticket purchases in the fall of 1996, so that by spring 1998 they had two-and-a-half years of information with which to work. By far, the biggest group of "dropouts" was added to the mailing list before 1996 but have not purchased tickets since. In some cases, these names were added to the company's list on the rec-ommendations of friends or by trading mailing lists with other companies.

Obviously, these 1,874 names—fifty-nine percent of those on the mailing list—are nonactive patrons who cost a considerable amount of money with no return on the investment. Because it has been so long since these people purchased tickets, it may be likely that most can't be turned into active patrons.

Two Courses of Action

Because of recent postal hikes, plus the increasing cost of printing promotional mailers, the company has decided to purge inactive pa-trons from its mailing list. Two options present themselves:

1. *Remove all inactive names without notification.* This would be the easiest and least-expensive route, but there is always the possibility that some people may not have been updated to active status by mistake. In this case, a further concern is that the company sells tickets at a local store and at the box office, and in neither case records the name of the purchaser. Some of the "inactives" could be from these groups.

2. *Send a special mailing to all nonactive patrons asking them if they wish to remain on the mailing list.* This means producing and mailing about eighteen hundred pieces. The company would then purge its list of all those who don't respond. The cost for printing and mailing the least-expensive piece would be $400, so the question is whether it is worth the cost, considering the number of "active" patrons this option would flush out.

Recent Dropouts

If cost is a major concern, the focus should be shifted to those pa-trons who purchased tickets in 1996 or 1997 but haven't since. These dropouts provide a greater potential for reinvolvement with the com-pany. In such a case, the following letter might do the trick:

Dear Mr. and Mrs. Smith:

We've missed you! It's been a while since you've been to one of our shows, and we just wanted to let you know how much we'd like to have you back as one of our regular patrons. As a token of our appreciation for your past support, we've enclosed a special coupon that entitles you to two tickets for the price of one for our upcoming production. Simply enclose the coupon if you order by mail or give the coupon number when you order tickets by phone.

We look forward to seeing you again.

Amy Lowell
President

The Bottom Line

Remember, your mailing list is probably your single most important vehicle for selling tickets. If you spend money on any kind of promotion, this should take priority. If money is short, you would be better off not cutting back in other areas (paid ads, for example); instead, concentrate on building and maintaining your loyal audience.

Of course, your mailing list will continue to grow. However, each year you can send a mailing to those who have not attended in the past two years. Once the company in question purges those eighteen hundred inactive patrons, future mailings to the dropouts will cost considerably less.

Keeping your mailing list restricted to active patrons takes effort, but it can save you a great deal of money over the long haul.

36 | Keeping Your Audience: Did You Know?

Holding on to Your Subscribers

The Sacramento Theatre Company's support group, Applause, hosted its fifth annual subscriber open house. The event, scheduled for a Monday at 5:30 P.M., was billed as "a special evening to discover *your* theatre." Among other activities, the open house included an introduction to the 1990–91 season by the company's artistic director, wine and hors d'oeuvres in the lobby, door prizes, and a backstage tour that included props, costumes, set construction, rehearsal area, and administrative offices. This provides a wonderful forum for subscribers to ask questions and is an excellent way to build strong relationships with season-ticket holders.

Don't Forget

Remember that it costs less money to get your current audience to return than it does to entice new patrons into your theater. Always treat existing patrons at least as well as you treat new ones.

A Helping Hand

Assist your patrons ᴜ   ᴄing large signs at the box office or in your lobby to help them know what to do. You could post, for instance, "This line for ticket sales only" or "Prepaid Pickup Window" or "$9 regular, $7 students and seniors." Anyone who has ever stood in the wrong line at a checkout counter, post office, or bank will appreciate what such an effort can do.

Eat Up

South Coast Repertory in Costa Mesa, California, offers subscribers a Restaurant Bonus Program. Seven restaurants participate, offering discounts or a free course when you order two or more entrees and show your SCR ticket for that day's performance. SCR encourages its subscribers to attend a different restaurant each time they visit the theater.

Backstage Bonus

North Carolina's Raleigh Little Theatre offers a Backstage Night for all its members, old and new. "Come on over and get the scoop on all the fall shows (or get the latest dirt on your friends)," explains the newsletter. "There will be tours and games to test your mettle. Sign up to work back stage, in the costume shop, in the office, as ushers—anywhere you'd like. And of course, refreshments will be served."

Just Rewards

Having problems getting audiences to a lesser-known production or a play festival? Make admission free or at a discount for those attending one of your regular season or better-known shows. The Ensemble Theatre of Cincinnati granted free admission to its Young Playwrights' Festival for those purchasing a ticket to the mainstage production of *Death of a Salesman*. (Tickets to the festival were $5 at the door.) Because the festival allows student writers the opportunity to see their work as full-scale productions, the free tickets to Ensemble Theatre patrons helped ensure an audience for these new plays. Patrons also felt rewarded for their attendance at the mainstage production.

Visual Aid

While an increasing number of theaters now offer audio systems or sign-language interpreters for hearing-impaired audience members, the Driftwood Players, in Edmonds, Washington, have gone a step further in making their productions accessible to all. For their first show this past season, the Players offered their sight-impaired audience members programs printed in Braille.

Sweet Spot

Texas' Henderson County Performing Arts Center is betting that audience members for its production of *A Christmas Carol* have a sweet tooth. During intermission of the show, the company runs its Sweets Auction, where patrons get to bid on goodies baked and prepared by theater volunteers. In addition to being a good fundraiser, it's also an audience-pleaser.

In on the Plan

Each year, the Village Theatre in Issaquah, Washington, asks donors, subscribers, and randomly selected single-ticket buyers to help the company "formulate our future seasons and give us a report card on how we're doing." According to the company newsletter, it received eleven hundred responses during a recent year. That is an impressive result.

While that survey showed that most theatergoers were happy with the mix of offerings, a similar survey by the Market House Theatre in Paducah, Kentucky, indicated that its audiences wanted more musicals and comedies. As a result, the theater's thirtieth anniversary season featured two musicals and three comedies. Based on survey results, MHT also removed the December family show from its season package and is offering it as a bonus production with more matinees and earlier evening performances.

Don't Alienate

When a caller asked about ticket availability, the answer was, "I can give you four nice seats in the orchestra section." There was a pause. "Well," the caller said, hesitating, "we'd really rather sit with the audience." Even if the ticket person explained the term *orches-*

tra, the caller very likely felt a little foolish when it was all done. And the last thing any theater wants to do is to alienate people— particularly those who are already interested in coming to your shows. A good rule is that before you recommend seating, ask, "Are you familiar with our theater?" If the caller says "yes," you probably can recommend orchestra seats. If the caller says "no," switch to something more generic, such as "downstairs center, about six rows back."

IN THE SPOTLIGHT
These Theaters Have Fought the Fight

S ometimes, the best way to learn how to attract and keep audiences is to learn how specific theaters have done exactly that. You may understand the theory, yet wonder how the theory operates in real life. In looking at particular circumstances, you can see which tactics would apply to your own situation, and which techniques would not be useful to you.

In each issue of *Stage Directions*, we "spotlight" one particular theater that we feel has some lessons to offer the rest of us. Whether a high school or college program, a community theater or a regional company, the *SD* spotlight is designed to illuminate common concerns and desires as well as solutions.

Over the next several chapters, we take a look at some very different theaters that have had to directly confront the question of audience attraction and retention, and have managed to significantly increase their audiences and keep those patrons with techniques any theater company may be able to use.

37 | *Keeping the Lamp Lighted*

"**W**e can already tell we are bringing in a new crowd; so many people say they've never been here before," says Alan Harvey of San Francisco's The Lamplighters.

A new crowd? That's a dream come true for most theater companies. How has The Lamplighters, a group with thirty-six years of experience, found this new audience? Harvey, general director of the company, which originally was founded to produce the works of Gilbert & Sullivan, explains: "We've never done much advertising. Our board of directors is resistant to it, claiming that we never needed it, that old methods have always worked. They've had to rethink."

This rethinking had been the direct result of a decline in attendance over the past two years, even though publicity has been excellent, including a strong direct-mail program. Harvey attributes this drop to two major factors: the aging of the Lamplighter audience and the impact of home video. The latter, he believes, has hurt live theater everywhere.

Shunning any Band-Aid approaches, The Lamplighters began, properly, by getting in expert help, including a Business Volunteers for the Arts (BVA) marketing volunteer. This volunteer has given the group a long-range marketing plan that will include application for grant money to fund it. Meanwhile, some short-term solutions have been put into effect.

"About ten to fifteen years ago, we began doing an occasional non-G&S show," Harvey says. "We've done *Something's Afoot, Ernest in Love,* and our recent production of *Of Thee I Sing*—shows that have much the same spirit as the Gilbert & Sullivan comic operas."

The problem, he says, is finding musicals that don't require a large dancing chorus or complex sets and lighting, narrowing the selection considerably.

Before venturing into "unknown territory," however, The Lamplighters took the sensible step of surveying their patrons. Audiences were asked how long they had been coming to the Lamplighters productions and to name both their favorite and least favorite show by the company.

The survey revealed that forty-three percent favored doing one non-G&S period piece a season, while fifty-seven percent were for the status quo (Gilbert & Sullivan and other comic opera). This indicated that the company should not move too far afield, at least at present.

Recently, the company has considered *She Loves Me* and *The Boys from Syracuse,* among other more modern shows. These not only "provide a stretch for the performers," Harvey explains, but also draw a wider audience than Gilbert & Sullivan fans. The most likely combination for their seasons would be two G&S productions and one Broadway show.

Meanwhile, if new audiences don't always come to its shows, The Lamplighters will go to them, in the form of small traveling shows that make money for the company and help get its name out. These "potpourris" are advertised in the program for each show; sometimes people simply phone the company to find out if anything is available.

Until the full marketing plan is developed and implemented, such short-term approaches will continue to be tested. So far, results seem encouraging. However, as Harvey points out, "It's hard to tell if what's happening is the result of our activities or some other variable."

We think he echoes the feelings of many of those involved in community theater. We'd like to think that all we need is to be good and audiences will flock to see us. However, as the Mikado says, "It's an unjust world . . . and virtue is triumphant only in theatrical performances."

38 | *A Gem of an Idea: How the Jewel Box Sells Out*

NANCIANNE PFISTER

We're usually not so foolish as to say, "Now we've heard everything," but we came close recently while asking our readers how they promoted their shows. Charles Tweed, Production Director at Oklahoma City's Jewel Box Theatre, gave us a surprising answer.

"We don't have to advertise at all. We sell out ninety-eight percent of every show. If we do any more publicity, it really harms us because people call for tickets and there are none."

If you're feeling less than sympathetic, you're not alone. Reader reactions to Jewel Box's plight were predictable. "We should all have such troubles," "Poor things," "Tough bounce," and "Yeah, sure" were among the printable. But the most predictable and frequent response was, "How do they do it?" Tweed explains.

"During my third year here, we needed a gimmick," he recalls, "something to increase the number of season-ticket holders. I went to the board of directors and asked that the price of a season ticket be lowered from $13 to $10 for six shows. I told them we should just pick up the tab."

An outrageous idea? Of course. The price change took

place in the early 1980s, but even by monetary standards of those days, few people could fail to see that $13 for six shows is already a bargain. Why should the chance to save $3 more be a big motivator to people who had not previously purchased season tickets?

"We gave people a good reason to do what they wanted to do anyway," says Tweed. They must have. The number of season-ticket holders soared from 237 to 958. The very act of lowering ticket prices was newsworthy and created a wave of publicity all its own. The phenomenon caught the attention of the Oklahoma Community Theatre Association, the American Association of Community Theatre picked up the story, and eventually the *New York Times* ran an article on the instant growth. Jewel Box has enjoyed a steady increase of 150 to two hundred patrons a season and now boasts more than three thousand subscribers. Costs rise and so must ticket fees—usually. The current season-ticket price is $30 for six shows, three of which are musicals.

Jewel Box Theatre has been around for nearly forty seasons, so it's clear there is more to its success than bargain prices. After all, even fifty cents is too much to pay for a *bad* show, and audiences who are disappointed are audiences who do not return. Companies thrive by earning the confidence of their audiences. Consistency sells and Tweed brags that the quality of Jewel Box productions is maintained.

"Our audiences trust us," claims Tweed. "We have good directors and they give us good shows. If I look back on any five years of our operation, I'll see that in four out of five of those years, all six shows have been good. Also, our audiences are open to seeing unfamiliar shows. When we announce our season, some people call to say, 'I don't know any of these shows, but I'll renew anyway.' " Some of that trust was handed back the year Jewel Box allowed its audience to dictate the choice of productions.

"We push giveaway tickets on the radio and have comps for cast members. The papers generally do a preshow feature story on one of the people in the show. It might be a choreographer who has never worked with us or a director who's been with us a lot. We have to be careful not to do too much and then disappoint people when there are no more tickets. We sell out a week in advance and then the final week is hell in the lobby as people fight to get on the waiting list."

The two hundred-seat theater-in-the-round originally was built as choir space for a church. Later, the theater became so successful that the choir moved out and the theater company now rents the space from the church.

Because of its association with the church, Jewel Box has

traditionally produced family shows. Tweed is quick to point out that "family entertainment" does not mean "bland" and notes such challenging productions as *Wait Until Dark, Steel Magnolias, 'Night, Mother*, and *South Pacific.*

Jewel Box's usual season runs from September through May. In June a few years ago, the company produced *Joseph and the Amazing Technicolor Dreamcoat.* The production was mounted in an outdoor amphitheater that had stood unused and deteriorating on the church grounds for twenty-five years. Because there had been little publicity beyond word-of-mouth, Tweed did not anticipate great response to the event.

"The amphitheater seats three thousand. I ordered five hundred programs for the four-night run of the show. The first night we needed 550. Thank heaven for Kinko's! Next we moved back into our theater for a benefit run of *Nunsense.* We made $6,000 to $10,000 in two weeks. Then we went back outdoors to the amphitheater for a two-weekend run of *South Pacific.*

"Maybe your readers will get some ideas from our experience," says Tweed. "You think you can't cut prices, but maybe you're wrong." Tweed cautions, however, against thinking a full house will end all your problems.

"Just because you're sold out doesn't mean everything's hunky-dory. Not a week goes by that someone isn't complaining because they can't get in. They come on the wrong night and are mad because we're sold out. It's tough to be at the high end of the box office too." *Now* we've heard everything.

How Ya Gonna Keep 'Em? Sioux Falls Knows!

39

NANCIANNE PFISTER

*A*ny theater company whose mission statement includes both *amateur* and *high-quality* must be doing something right. You probably know that the difference between *amateur* and *professional* is more than a matter of who gets paid; it also describes an attitude. To declare an actor *amateur* is to invoke the Latin verb *amo* meaning *I love*. The amateur performs for the love of doing so. In this sense, it seems clear that many highly paid professionals are truly amateurs in their soul.

"My philosophy is that we amateurs must operate as a professional theater company," says Ron Ziegler, formerly the Artistic/Managing Director of South Dakota's Sioux Falls Community Playhouse. "That's the way to provide the high quality that kept people in Sioux Falls, not drifting off to Rapid City or to Minneapolis."

Not only does the Playhouse have to be concerned with keeping an audience, it also must keep the 350 to four hundred volunteers who contribute time, money, and energy to the success of the company each year. Ziegler was one of only seven paid staff. In most businesses, decisions are usually made by those earning the biggest salaries. In a volunteer organization, the major decisions may be made by people who get no salary at all. It takes a little mind adjusting, according to Ziegler.

"The company was founded by volunteers," he says, "but I was hired to direct my employers. Without those volunteers, we'd be dead, so we do what we can to keep them happy and coming back to us. Our volunteers want to be associated with a company that does high-quality shows; they help bring in our audience."

That audience comes from Sioux Falls—population 110,000—and the surrounding area of 160,000. Playhouse productions were enjoyed by more than forty-four thousand people last year. To reward the community for such support, the Playhouse strives to keep its money in the town; ninety-one percent of all expenditures are made in Sioux Falls. Because of the high quality of Playhouse shows, residents are less apt to take their money two hundred miles east to the St. Paul/Minneapolis theaters or three hundred miles west to Rapid City, thus keeping an estimated $120,000 in the city.

Additionally, the presence of the Playhouse generates income for restaurants and other businesses. (Ziegler is the first person to talk to us about money brought into the city by his theater. Other companies tell us only about the artistic influence they have on their communities. Would it be a good idea for your company to let it be known—especially during fundraising—that you produce not only a cultural benefit, but also have some bottom-line commercial value to the place where you live?)

"We got some degree of migration," says Ziegler of his experience in Sioux Falls, noting that the city had no facility that can accommodate a technically complicated national touring show. "A touring company played *Cats* in Rapid City. They have a performance center for it; we didn't." Why not?

"There is a general sentiment that we need a performing-arts center, but it was a ten-year struggle. Right downtown is Washington High School, built in the 1930s. It would make a fine omni theater, with space for art and a museum too. Plans were under way, but then there was sudden opposition to the renovation. This is a progressive community, but they are cautious with public money. If people understood, they'd be all for it.

"To build a new, free-standing performance center would cost an estimated $18 million. A renovation of the old high school would cost over $21 million, but we'd have three times the space and would turn a profit. Given the economic impact on the region, it would soon pay for itself."

The Playhouse knows something about renovation; their charming 688-seat auditorium was built in 1913 as a vaudeville house and was later used as a movie theater. In 1975, shop space was added. A 1983 restoration project added some cosmetic amenities, as well as a new scene house (fly system and stage floor). In 1991, the Playhouse renovated its office areas. A recent season included *Godspell, Private Lives, Dancing at Lughnasa, Prelude to a Kiss,* and *City of Angels.* General season tickets are a bargain at $54 and a subscription entitles the ticket-holder to discount rates at workshops and special presentations.

Asked how he was able to obtain rights to *Dancing at Lughnasa* so soon after its Broadway run, Ziegler allowed that there are advantages to geographic isolation. "Because we weren't a major city, we sometimes got rights early. There was little competition, since the nearest resident company is over two hundred miles away. I just called Dramatists Play Service (which holds the rights) and was kind of surprised when they said 'Yes.' "

The last fifteen years have seen major growth in Playhouse activities. The Education Program of adult theater workshops began in 1984 and resulted in the two-play Studio Series. A year later, Youth Education Program (YEP) came into being with children's classes and plays. YEP has grown to include a dozen classes each semester, four drama daycamps each summer, and a four-show Children's Series. Add a Christmas show and the annual fundraiser musical and it's not surprising that the Playhouse outgrew its home. The Actors Studio is an off-site rented facility that houses classrooms and rehearsal space.

Recent evidence of the high quality that keeps audiences returning to Sioux Falls Community Playhouse came when the Playhouse production of *Other People's Money,* after winning state and regional competitions, was chosen to represent the seven-state Region 5 at the American Association of Community Theatre Festival.

Congratulations. What a great bunch of amateurs!

40 | Meeting the Challenge

Alabama's Mobile Theatre Guild Prospers with New Works

NANCIANNE PFISTER

G etting an audience for one new play is a challenge to most theater companies. Now imagine having to sell an *entire season* of new works or plays that otherwise might not be seen locally.

That's what Alabama's Mobile Theatre Guild does year after year—and quite successfully, thank you.

How does MTG do it? One way is by including one familiar (but not often produced) show to finance the rest of the season.

A recent Guild season opened with *Ruthless! The Musical*, followed by the holiday show, *Greetings*. The winter was warmed by *Smoke on the Mountain*, and March saw *Waiting for the Parade*. In May, the season closed with *A Few Good Men*.

Does it work? Yes, for the most part. While acknowledging that MTG rarely sells out a run, especially of a drama, Michael McKee, resident managing director, boasts of discerning—and loyal—season subscribers.

"Here in Mobile, theatergoing is primarily a social event," he explains. "People go to be with friends and have a social evening. Our lobby is about the size of most people's bathrooms, so there's no room to socialize. People who come to us come to see a play."

McKee found out the hard way that any perception that the company is condescending to its audience (and thus denying MTG's unique educational benefits) is a shortcut to disaster.

"One year, just to be more commercial, we included *Plaza Suite* in the season," recalls McKee. "It was a mistake. Our regulars didn't show; they made it clear they would not come to us for the kind of show they could see elsewhere. And we didn't draw new people from the other theaters."

While at one time MTG was one of only two community theaters in town, now within a ten-mile radius of the city are four community theaters, three college theaters, and one professional company. Those other theaters compete for the same talent pool and arts dollars.

MTG must distinguish itself, as it has done since it was founded as the Catholic Theatre Guild by Reverend Anthony Zoghby in 1950. Father Zoghby's general advice to players was, "Learn your lines and be good." Performances were held in a building on church grounds. Today, the 150-seat theater MTG enjoys rent-free is owned by the Diocese of Mobile. In most cities, when a theater displeases patrons, the ticket-buyers complain to city hall; at MTG, the disgruntled phone the bishop.

A thirty-member board of directors works to prevent such disgruntlement and to advance the company's overall mission. Thirty people may seem an unwieldy number, but McKee maintains it is a true working board. There are members-at-large who have special projects, and members responsible for every aspect of the company, from selecting plays (which include scripts by Alabama playwrights) to raising funds. And board members clean the theater before each show.

A few years ago, the cast and crew of the Mobile production, *Marvin's Room*, including director McKee, returned from Dundalk, Ireland, where they earned fourth-place honors and three individual awards in an international amateur theater festival: two for acting and one for set design. Was the trip worth the money? McKee sees benefits to MTG beyond the fleeting glory. "We have many new patrons and sponsors. The Ireland trip led to new corporate involvement. They came initially to help us get to Dundalk, but a great many businesses have stayed with us. And we learned so much from the workshops. We found new shows we could produce and we made valuable international contacts. And we got a lot of new fundraising ideas."

Those ideas, no doubt, will help finance the production of the next little-known script by an obscure Alabama playwright.

Final Words

While we rehearse and prepare away from the roar of the crowd, we rehearse and prepare *for* the crowd. Although we may stand on stage alone, theater is, after all, an interactive art; we need an audience.

As, in fact, the first interactive art, it predates video games and computer simulations by millennia. For it to continue to be successful in the new millennium of video games and computers, we must use every means at our disposal to find new and old audiences, to entice them to watch, and to make sure they come back.

Let us know if you have any additional thoughts on how to do this.

Contributors

MICHAEL CAFFERKY, a community theater performer, has provided marketing consultation services for services companies for nearly two decades.

DIANE CREWS is Executive/Artistic Director of DreamWrights Youth & Family Theatre, in York, Pennsylvania.

LISA LAWMASTER HESS is a freelance writer based in York, Pennsylvania.

MICHAEL KANTER served as executive director of Theater Marketing Services, an audience development firm located in San Diego.

DOUGLAS LARCHE is chair of the Department of Speech and Theatre Arts at Grand View College in Des Moines, Iowa, and a published playwright.

STEPHEN PEITHMAN is co-founder and Editor-in-Chief of *Stage Directions*.

NANCIANNE PFISTER is Associate Editor of *Stage Directions*.

TERRI RIOUX writes business brochures, newsletters, and articles for magazines from her home in Connecticut.

NANCY ROTHMAN, who lives in New York, served as marketing manager for Harper & Row, Harcourt Brace, Jovanovich, and NewsBank.

SARAH STARR is a freelance writer now living in Nacogdoches, Texas.

MORE BOOKS
from Heinemann's *Stage Directions* series

Stage Directions Guide to Auditions
Edited by Stephen Peithman and Neil Offen

This book is different from other audition books in that it addresses the needs of both actors who are auditioning and directors who are conducting the auditions. It's filled with practical advice for making the most of the audition process, including information on how to prepare, audition procedures, tips for holding auditions, callbacks, memorable monologues, and much more!

0-325-00083-2 / 144pp / 1998

Stage Directions Guide to Publicity
Edited by Stephen Peithman and Neil Offen

The key to getting people into your theatre is getting the word out about it. But if your theatre isn't on Broadway and doesn't have an expensive press agent (or an extensive ad budget), how does it get attention? This book has the answers, including information on what draws an audience to a show, how to improve your mailing pieces, tips for more effective ads, and many other aspects of the publicity game.

0-325-00082-4 / 144pp / 1999

Stage Directions Guide to Directing
Edited by Stephen Peithman and Neil Offen

Every director—from the beginner to the most experienced—will find in this book invaluable information to make their direction more effective. Topics covered include things to look for in an audition, selecting the right play, criticizing effectively, basics of directing a musical, staging a big show with a small cast, blocking tips, managing rehearsals and schedules, and much more!

0-325-00112-X / 168pp / Available May 1999

For more information about these books,
visit us on-line at **www.heinemanndrama.com**,
call 800-793-2154, fax 800-847-0938,
or write: Heinemann, Promotions Dept., 361 Hanover St., Portsmouth, NH 03801.